The Serenity Experiment

Searching for Personal Peace
in a World That Won't Slow Down

David Howell

BLUE EAR BOOKS

Published in 2021 by
Blue Ear Books
7511 Greenwood Ave N, Box 400
Seattle, WA 98103
USA

blueearbooks.com

ISBN: 978-0-9990951-6-4

Credits:

Cover Art:
  Kaitlyn Howell
Cover Design:
  Robin Lewis
Book Composition:
  Jennifer Haywood, Blue Ear Books

CONTENTS

All of humanity's problems stem from man's inability to sit quietly in a room alone.

— Blaise Pascal

PART ONE

Sitting Still in a Pandemic

1.

I'm sitting at a picnic table, at the edge of the Milwaukee River, at a park a few miles from home. It feels good to get out of the house. Sue, my wife, and I haven't left home much for a few months. The governor's "stay in place" dictum provided guidance, how to safely navigate our way through the pandemic: Try not to leave your home, and when you do, wear a mask, practice social distancing, and keep washing your hands.

I stopped going to work once my university's president shut the campus down, once courses went online. For the past ten weeks, I've been teaching out of our basement, staring into a laptop most of the day.

Which is why this park is needed. Not long ago, the park was closed. Now it's full of folks walking their dogs, pushing baby strollers, out for a jog. No one wears a protective face mask. Folks stop and chat within feet of each other. It's as if everyone is willfully ignoring the pandemic, simply pretending that life is as it was.

I'm trying to get my head wrapped around the idea that there is no returning to life as it was, that this pandemic has changed everything forever, that the world we now live in is prone to pandemics. It's why I'm struggling with the people in this park. They behave as if nothing has happened, yet it is happening all around us. It doesn't help that it's a virus, something we cannot see. You watch the news at night and view the daily statistics, how many people have contracted COVID-19 and how many are dying from it. If you know someone who contracted it, if you're within one degree of separation, it's real. Otherwise, it seems ethereal.

Riots are breaking out in Minneapolis/St. Paul because a police officer strangled George Floyd with his knee. My daughter, Kait, lives a mile from the epicenter of the riots. We talk on the phone regularly so she can reassure me that she's being smart, that she and her partner, Sophie, have an escape strategy if things get hot. The arresting officer was finally charged with third-degree murder and manslaughter. Who knows how this will affect the unrest.

While that's happening, Sue's trying to keep her small business afloat, reopening her wholistic veterinary practice. But how does she go about seeing animals when their owners want to participate in the examination? She's figured out a method: curbside pickup of the pet, enable the owner to use Zoom to view the examination, bill them online. Every night she comes home exhausted, not from the work so much as from having to do it in a way that protects everyone who is involved in her business. Some clients just walk in, no mask and no worries: They don't believe the pandemic is real. When Sue tells them to step out of the clinic and return to their vehicles, they get angry.

And then there's Evan, my son, a recent college graduate who has decided to make a go of it in Portland. He's trying to find a job during record unemployment. He didn't have a job when he was a student, so he can't file for unemployment. He's always been stressed over his studies; now he must learn how to navigate the anxieties of "real life."

None of this seems real. More surreal, dystopic. My response is to sit here, on a park bench, try not to judge people for their behavior, and watch the river go by. This river, and the silence engendered when focused on the river, will be the center of my attention.

2.

I've been planning for a while now to establish the ritual of sitting on park benches. Every day a new park and a new picnic table. Yesterday it was in Thiensville; today, it's a bench in Estabrook Park, on the north side of Milwaukee. I leave the house on my bike after completing the morning rituals with Sue: coffee in bed and conversation for about an hour, walk the dog around the neighboring nature preserve, breakfast and more coffee, and then, and only then, hopping on a bike to find a new place to sit still for a while.

The academic school year ended last week. Now I enjoy the three best reasons to be a university professor: June, July, and August. I have always had summers off; I'm usually trying to find a side job to make some money and help pay for everyone's college education. For the last four years, I've contributed to Evan's college fund; before that, it was Kait's fund; and before that, I was paying off student loans for Sue and me. I was in college for thirteen years, racking up a quarter of a million dollars in debt. I loved being a college student, being in an environment designed around learning. I love being a professor: Now I get paid to be in a learning environment, and what I make helps pay for my children's college educations.

This is the first summer I'm away from work, which is why it's ironic that I'm actually working right now. I applied for a summer grant so I can write a book for my ethics class. Is it work, sitting on a park bench, enjoying the sun, counting dandelions? I want to write

5

a book that explains to my students that sitting down on a summer afternoon is an ethical choice, something "good" to do. It just seems ironic that I'm getting paid to do this: that when I finally have the opportunity to not work, I find a way to work anyway.

I have an ongoing argument with my students. They tell me they can't wait to graduate, to stop working so hard on their studies, to get a job that's not as intellectually taxing or demanding of their time. I tell them it's a ruse: that they're taking the best years of their life, from eighteen to twenty-one, and using them to learn how to work, work, work. Once you learn how to do that, it's difficult to unlearn. It simply becomes part of what you do: four years of no-stop habituated undergraduate behavior.

It's a concern that I have for Evan. I'm proud of the fact that he's a hard worker, a great student. But looking for a job when there are not many jobs out there is a different kind of labor. You can't solve the problem by working harder, which is how he's always solved problems.

I'm at a different place on the learning curve. Writing an ethics text such as this doesn't feel "hard." I've been thinking about these ideas for so long that they just arrive when I draft lesson plans. Content streams from my lectures with an appearance of spontaneity because I've delivered the lectures every semester for over a decade. And even though I keep lecturing and discussing all topics related to ethics, I never seem to grow tired of it. It's a branch of philosophy that keeps morphing, as long as you're willing to change with it.

In the spirit of not making this project too hard to do, I choose to do it in parks—solitude, picnic tables, summer afternoons. I tell my students that "easy is good," that if it's easy for them to write down their ideas, it'll probably be easy for the audience to read them. So I will make this process as easy as possible.

I love riding my bike, being outside, meeting the challenge of trying to sit still. Why not bring them all together while doing something that's apparently difficult: drafting a course text for an ethics class?

Ethics is difficult: determining right from wrong, then acting in such a way that you do what's right, what's good.

Another reason I want to spend the summer sitting in local parks is to see what it does to my thought process. Five years ago, I bicycled from Seattle to Milwaukee and kept a journal, so I could document the thoughts I was having during the ride. it was a great thought experiment: I discovered that the more time and space I had to think, the more depth my thoughts acquired.

I enjoy thinking deeply, delving into a concept further and further, but doing so requires time and space. The more time and space you have, the deeper thought can go.

That bike ride was fun because I traveled solo. I had thirty-two days of somewhat uninterrupted thought. The thought experiment I'm currently enacting is domestic: when I'm done sitting in a park, I return home, and home is full of other things I need to think about.

Toward the end of the month-long bike ride, when cycling through Minnesota, I ran into Jake, a fellow bicycle tourer who was cycling from Portland to Minneapolis. Like me, he was traveling solo. And, like me, he kept a journal to track his thoughts. We talked about how the journey provides the opportunity for reflection, especially toward the end of the journey. The trick, I said, is to figure out how to ritualize these opportunities for reflection in our daily domestic lives. Jake disagreed. He said the trick is always to go on long reflective journeys.

It's my hope that sitting on these park benches day after day, week after week, will replicate the experience I had on that big bike ride.

Physically, I'm not traveling far from home. The spaces I inhabit are familiar. Part of the pleasure of bike touring is that everything is new: Every time you go down a road, it's your first time down that road. It's why I enjoy travel writing, or traveling in general:

Everything is always new, stimulating, somewhat unexpected. I enjoy travel writing because it's easy: The material presents itself. You don't have to look for it. Alain de Botton wrote that the "pleasure we derive from journeys is perhaps dependent more on the mindset with which we travel than on the destination we travel to." So this is a series of interconnected hypotheses that need to be tested: Will sitting on these benches, in these parks, present the opportunity to journey, to see the unexpected? Is there drama in sitting still and watching what happens in these green spaces? Will it hold my attention, and as a result, expand it?

The scale is different: Instead of watching black bears wander through a campground foraging for food, I watch squirrels jumping from tree to tree, or I watch robins hunting for worms. People love it when I tell bear stories—the time a bear hit my bike, or the time a bear sat outside my tent all night. They don't react the same way when I talk about the yellow finches that eat from the bird feeders in my backyard.

Still, I'm reminded of something I learned in a creative writing class I took a decade ago: you can climb a hundred mountains, or you can climb the same mountain a hundred times. The professor shared this pearl of wisdom with us as a way of encouraging us to find the uncommon in the common, not to rely on the drama to come to us but instead to find the drama that's already present. A good writer, the professor said, will make it dramatic, will give the scene meaning, regardless of what action takes place.

I think about this as I think about living an ethical life, pursuing the good. Doing good sounds boring in comparison to delving into nefarious behavior. But what is boredom? And do we have to neglect what is "good" for the sake of entertaining ourselves? Can sitting in a park be as enticing as bicycling across the country?

There is a key difference between what I'm doing now and what I did five years back. On that big bike ride, the focus was on cycling and thinking. Now, cycling is simply a vehicle for arriving at a park so I can sit and think. Yes, you sit on a bicycle, but sitting at a park bench is different. You aren't moving, so you need to pay attention to what moves around you.

About an hour ago, a mother and her son bicycled up to some maple trees. They parked the bikes, and the mother hung a couple of hammocks. They took out books and read. Does this make for good drama? From where I'm sitting, it looks like good parenting, encouraging your child to read—modeling reading—in hammocks, in the shade of maple trees.

Watching them spend time together is good. It's good to stop and recognize what is good.

3.

I'm at a park in Cedarburg, two townships north of home. The park has a small lake and ample picnic tables. I'm sitting at one near the lake's edge watching killdeer skim over the water, feeding on water skimmers. It's Saturday, and the park is full of people. Behind me two teenage girls listen to pop music on their radio, dance, and talk and laugh at full volume. In the background, I hear kids playing baseball at the other end of the park—the sound of aluminum bats hitting balls, coaches yelling at players.

On my bike ride to the park, I passed a local college where, in the parking lot, they provide drive-through COVID-19 testing. I'm struggling to understand how National Guard troops dressed in full HAZMAT suits can conduct COVID testing while seven miles down the road kids play baseball. This isn't good.

I spend a lot of time thinking about what is "good", probably because I teach the ethics class. My job isn't to teach students what "good" is, but to help them find it on their own. The students write essays about what they learn, assignments I am required to grade: I determine if the students' writing is good or not. What's harder is getting the students to want to write "good" essays, to see the value in articulating, delving into, and defending an articulation of applied goodness.

I don't think the university is the best place to find out what "good" is, to learn about it by reading philosophical text and write about personal and professional values, ethics, and morals. The best place to learn about goodness is outside of the artificial boundaries of the classroom, where everything is a test, where every action is good or bad, right or wrong. Nishida Kitaro writes about how "good" is an extension of one's personality, how if you continually do "good," it simply becomes an extension of who you are. I enjoy requiring my students to read Nishida's *An Inquiry into the Good*, so we can discuss whether they view themselves as good people, whether what they do is good, whether they have a moral compass, and whether it determines the direction of their lives.

I discovered *An Inquiry into the Good* at a difficult time in my life. Sue had been accepted to veterinary school, and I decided to get a master's in education with the goal of teaching first-graders. We wanted to live in small-town America, and I figured that every small town needs veterinarians and grade-school teachers. I took two years of courses and enjoyed learning various pedagogical theories: Vygotsky's zone of proximal development, Foucault's panopticon. Then it came time for my final semester, when I would do a practicum and co-teach in an actual first-grade classroom. The teacher I was placed with was happy to have me help, because, as she told me on my first day, she had a side-job she wanted to focus on, and she needed me to teach her class. I had no idea what I was doing and was concerned that I wasn't ready to take the lead without supervision, but I figured I would give it a go since I had no other choice.

Then the students arrived. I was startled at how much energy first graders have. Diffuse energy. Children constantly moving in every direction. An hour into my first day, one little girl looked at me, said, "I miss my mommy!" and ran out of the classroom, down the hall, and out of the building.

This continued for eighteen days, and on the eighteenth day, I couldn't get out of bed. I was depressed, exhausted, empty. I couldn't continue to face all those little children, so I called in sick. The next day, I phoned in sick again and made an appointment with my university representative to meet the day after. And at that meeting, I quit.

No one was happy with this decision. Not my university representative, who told me that I needed to finish the practicum to get the degree and teaching certificate. Not the supervising teacher who needed me to teach so she could work her side-job. Not Sue, who knew as well as I did that I had racked up two years of student loans to get the degree, and that without the degree there was no career. Yet I knew it was beyond me, and I had to stop before it took what little energy I had left.

Several weeks later I got a job at the university bookstore, shelving books. It was a good gig; it didn't require me to think. I was tired of thinking, of feeling. This job didn't require me to work with other people. Every day I'd show up, gather inventory, and shelve.

A month into the job, I shelved Nishida's book. It looked interesting: twentieth-century Japanese philosophy. I'd read a great deal of Japanese and Chinese poetry while pursuing a previous graduate degree and had dabbled in Buddhist philosophy. I couldn't afford to buy the book, so I would grab a copy and read it during lunch breaks. I wasn't accustomed to reading original philosophical text, especially text written in translation, but the ideas in this book began to resonate. Nishida's spin on William James's concept of pure experience. How Nishida equates love with knowledge. I completed the book in a month, and as I delved into a rereading, I realized that I could use it as the theoretical cornerstone for a doctoral thesis.

A month later, I submitted an application for the university's individual interdisciplinary doctoral program and was accepted. My life had completely turned around, going from defeat to reinvention, from drifting to moving forward, from bad to good, away from who I wasn't and toward who I suddenly wanted to become: a graduate student of philosophy, a subject-matter expert on Nishida Kitaro and the school of philosophy that he created, the Kyoto School.

At the time, I had no idea that Nishida's book would alter the trajectory of my life. At the time it was a lifeline, a way to get out of a desperate situation—lack of definition, purposelessness, debt—and move into a new space that provided purpose, opportunity, and impact. I wasn't free of despair and debt; they are ongoing components of most doctoral programs. But the purposelessness was gone. I didn't know what I would do with a Ph.D., but at least I had something to pursue while Sue finished veterinary school, and that was good.

4.

I'm sitting on Lafayette Hill on the east side of Milwaukee, over-looking Lake Michigan. During these summer months, I meet a friend, Mark, for coffee and conversation. Every Monday morning at ten o'clock sharp. Normally, we sit outside a coffee shop at the bottom of the hill, but coffee shops within the city limits are closed until further notice—another casualty of the pandemic. Instead, we meet at a long bench at the top of the hill, not far from his apartment. He teaches the same classes I teach: Composition, Technical Communication, Eastern Literature. More important, he's a writer, a poet, and, like me, he works at his craft daily—at least during the summer months, when we don't have to balance writing with teaching.

We've had an interactive correspondence ever since the start of the pandemic. Our university decided to pivot quickly to all-online instruction. The jump was easy for me, since I had a career in high tech before working at the university, but Mark didn't have that history. He has a healthy distrust of technology in general. After all, how does technology help one write poetry? It can be argued (as he does argue) that technology impedes the poetic mindset: its thirst for speed, the ability of word processors to edit automatically, the loss of the pen in your hand as you write on the blank paper page.

Mark needed some help transitioning from teaching in a physical classroom to a virtual one, so I helped him through the process. I was happy to help. Mark's a good teacher: He wants his students to appreciate writing the way he appreciates writing, and the students we work with benefit from his instruction.

Like me, his degrees are in English, and like me, he loves reading and writing. I find fewer and fewer people who read and write with a sense of depth, which makes it more necessary to work at friendships with folks like Mark. He also has a passion for Japanese poetry, not just because he appreciates the brevity and clarity of poets like Basho and Issa, but because he worked as a journalist in Japan for over a decade. He understands the correlation between Japanese culture and literature. He is the only person I know who reads the same poets I read, which again makes him an important person in my life.

We share our writing with each other. He even served as an editor on my last failed book project. And, like me, he's a romantic. You almost need to be if you have an English degree.

A problem with specializing in English—like specializing in anything—is that it teaches you to think in a certain way. You care about things that most folks don't care about. Mark cares about grammar—the value in n-dashes, the healthy distain for exclamation marks (the prose should engender a text's emphasis, not its punctuation!). As a poet, he cares about line breaks, stanza length, internal rhyme schemes. It permeates not just his writing but his thinking and speech. He understands the power in a pregnant pause. He's just fun to talk to, because his rhetoric is poetic, engaging from the perspective of content and delivery.

English departments are in a state of decay. Universities are focusing on job placement rates for their graduates and emphasize degree tracks that translate to instant, gainful employment. I laugh when I tell my engineering students that I landed some great jobs when I graduated with an English degree: driving a delivery truck, operating a forklift, pushing a broom in a warehouse. They were great jobs because they enabled me to work with people who had no appreciation for English, or higher education for that matter. And that made me think long and hard about the quality of my education.

I love being an English major. I love going to my office and looking at my personal library. I can pull out any book and recall the time and place I read it, who I was then in contrast to who I am now. I read the marginal annotations and reflect on the highlighted passages. So much of what I know is captured in those books.

જ

I enjoyed my conversation with Mark, though as we talked I kept thinking about the library in my office at work. I asked him about the books that altered his life. He told me about the impact that Hesse's *Steppenwolf* had on him—*Really, anything written by Hesse* he said. In return, I told him about the influence that Kundera's *The Unbearable Lightness of Being* had on me. A couple of friends talking about ourselves by talking about what we've read. What's amazing is the amount of content that we had at our disposal when discussing books. I was able to go into great detail about Kundera's character Sabina and her disdain for flags and parades, her rejection of an ideology imposed on her by a communist regime, her being required to participate in communist May Day parades as a child, her frustration with people who blindly follow flag wavers. I talked about her as if she were a real person. It's testament to the quality of Kundera's fiction: to me, Sabina is real. Her fictious experiences have impacted my experiences.

I was getting cold and told Mark that I had to get back to riding the bike. We said our goodbyes, and I rode to my office at the university campus in downtown Milwaukee. I wanted to sit in the office and stare at my library.

It didn't take long to recognize Pirsig's *Zen and the Art of Motorcycle Maintenance*. There are several copies, mostly hardcover, but the first copy I purchased when I was a freshman in college is the one I reached for. The binding is held together with packing tape. A rubber band wraps the book to ensure none of the yellowed pages fall out. Handwritten notes abound, changing as my handwriting morphed over the years. It was the first book I ever read in college, the first book I ever read cover to cover, something I wouldn't have done if I hadn't been required to do so. I eventually had to upgrade to a hardcover edition because my ageing eyes could no longer handle the size of the pocket paperback's font.

It wasn't so much the content of the book as the time in my life when it read it. I was a second-term freshman in college. I had tested into a remedial English class in my first semester. The second semester was a composition course, and the professor used Pirsig's novel as a required text. I was intimidated by the book's thickness, 367 pages.

In high school, I avoided reading books by inventing fake texts. There was one book I remember making up. I titled it *The Fundamentals of Downhill Skiing*, by Bob Boogieman. I wrote a book report on it my sophomore year and received a C, then submitted the same book report my junior year and received a B.

I didn't think I was smart enough to read books. When I was in middle school, I was tested and found out I'm dyslexic. My dad told me that "Howells get C's." It was his way of saying that we weren't that smart, so we had best make up for it by working hard.

I didn't engage in the class discussions of Pirsig's book. I never said anything in class in fear of acknowledging that I didn't have anything intelligent to say. I enjoyed the book, at least the parts that focused on the motorcycle trip and motorcycle maintenance. I didn't understand then that "motorcycle" is a metaphor for "self": that we must maintain ourselves if we hope to run properly.

I'm grateful that this initial experience, reading Pirsig, was positive. I recall reading the last page, realizing that I may not have understood the book, but at least I finished it.

5.

I'm sitting on a back patio of a local coffee shop. Sue and I did an early morning ride together, and I peeled off to have more coffee and do some sitting. it's already hot—it will hit the low nineties today. Good to get the sitting done while I can comfortably sit outside. I don't care much for heat, am more of a cold weather person. It'll be nice to be in an air-conditioned house this afternoon, rereading the textbooks I plan to use when school starts up again in the fall.

I'll require my freshmen composition students to read *Zen and the Art of Motorcycle Maintenance*, which means I get to reread the book again. There are about a dozen books that I reread. The books don't change, but I seem to, because I always get something new out of each read. I like Pirsig's writing style, the dual-narrative approach to the book's storyline. The students tend to enjoy the parts about the motorcycle journey, a similar reading experience to what I had back in the day. A few students typically delve into the philosophical passages, Pirsig's Chautauqua on quality, the bits about Buddhism. It's a lot to ask of freshmen, especially in their first semester of college. But I was eventually transformed by the book; maybe some of them will be too.

I gifted a copy to Kait when she was in college. We never talked about it until we were on a bike tour three years ago, a month-long adventure that served as a graduation gift for the completion of her undergraduate degree. We took an Amtrak out to Spokane and rode

19

through Idaho, Washington, Oregon, and Montana. Like all bike tours, there were good days and bad days. At the end of one particularly bad day—a hot day like today, when we climbed several mountain passes in the North Cascades—I asked her why she had decided to do the tour. To my surprise, she quoted verbatim a passage from Pirsig: "Peace of mind produces right values, right values produce right thoughts. Right thoughts produce right actions and right actions produce work which will be a material reflection for others to see of the serenity at the center of it all."

She had read the book but hadn't told me. It gave us a chance to talk about it while biking around the Pacific Northwest, though we didn't talk about it often, probably because of my over-enthusiastic attitude about the novel and my desire for her to love it as much as I did. I did spend time reflecting on the passage she quoted, its emphasis on "peace of mind" and "right values," especially since I teach value creation in my ethics classes. I thought about the relationship between peace of mind and values and how that leads to right thoughts, actions, and good work. In my journal, I created a concentric circle paradigm.

In order to exercise good values, it helps to have peace of mind—serenity. My students are generally interested in the concept of serenity, but they explain its lack of presence in their lives. Ethics is a course you take right before you graduate. Seniors are wrapping up their tenure at a rigorous polytechnic institution, finishing up internships, applying for jobs, giving closure to year-long design projects—it doesn't leave much room for engendering serenity.

But the class isn't titled "Peace of Mind." Its focus instead is on ethics and how ethics should lead to right action. You follow the rules and behave accordingly—that's what most of the ethics textbooks I've read boil down to. I like this "Pirsig paradigm" because it has more nuance, more layers. Exercising values isn't the center of it all. Serenity is the center. And the more I've thought about this, the more it makes sense. If I'm serene, I have the perspective necessary to understand not only my values but the thoughts they engender, and that leads to right action. The only things people see are the work and actions: the externals. Only I have access to the thoughts, values, and serenity. Those inner rings are at the center.

I tell my students that their work is the manifestation of peace of mind, that all the circles are enacted simultaneously. They generally nod their heads in agreement, though I'm not convinced they reflect on this nearly as much as I want them to. Maybe it's because it's easier to focus on the externals, the actions one engages in to produce the work. Maybe it's because that's what potential employers focus on. After all, no one's going to pay you to be serene.

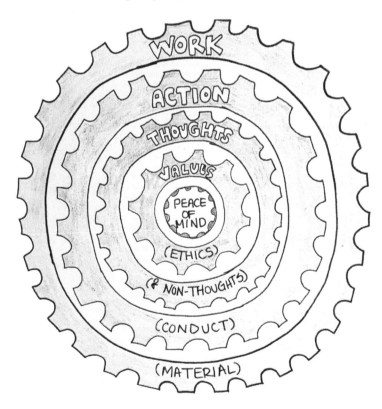

6.

I'm sitting at the base of an old maple tree, beside the Milwaukee River, in a small park with a boat launch where local fishermen can catch and release. I was planning on sitting at the one picnic table in the park, but there's a gaggle of Canadian geese around the table, and I'd rather not disturb them, having been chased by honkers in the past.

I'm troubled this morning. My brain isn't working well. Too much information making its way across the neural pathways. The intent of these daily trips to neighboring parks is to engender peace of mind. If it takes twenty-one days to establish a habit, then I'd like to intentionally sit in parks for at least twenty-one consecutive days with the expressed intent of habituating serenity. But I'm sure it doesn't work like that; it can't be that simple.

I need serenity right about now. I've developed the habit of watching the news so I can stay current on the pandemic and the George Floyd riots. I watched our president as he told representatives from the D.C. police and National Guard to smoke-bomb peaceful protesters so he, a sitting President of the United States, could conduct a photo op in front of a church. I saw the photo posted online this morning: he holds a Bible in the air, a stern facial expression. Earlier this week, he tweeted "When the looting starts, the shooting starts." It's difficult to comprehend that a president can behave this way. He's not the cause of the global pandemic; he did not choke George

Floyd to death. But he's certainly not helping the situation with his actions and rhetoric. I understand that divisiveness helps his cause. I get it. But it's difficult to witness.

We all need some serenity right about now. But first, there needs to be cultural anger and outrage. People need to be heard, and protesting is how you get someone to hear you when they refuse to do so.

7.

I couldn't write much yesterday, wasn't in the right mindset for sitting or writing. It requires mental silence and perspective, and I didn't have it. I want perspective today, more distance from my own thoughts, so I biked to a park on the bluff of Lake Michigan, to a picnic table in the shade of an evergreen. The bluff's been slowly eroding this spring; the table is feet from the cliff's edge. A view of the lake, a flat horizon of water, blue sky above blue lake.

I was watching the national news last night, and they had a clip of a Muslim teenage girl holding up a sign that read "Silence is violence." I turned off the television and thought about her message. I love silence, silence in nature, the lack of human voice so one can hear birds singing and bustling leaves. But this young woman's point, not speaking out against cultural, systemic racism—doing nothing is an act of doing—speaks to me.

I wish I were teaching ethics right now. That would provide me with a forum for discussion, to find out what students think of the protests. I taught them at the start of the pandemic; we had class on campus for a week before the university shut down to pivot to an online format. Once we were online, it was difficult to jumpstart the class discussion. Most students kept their cameras off and microphones muted. They were exercising distance, silence, the distance of virtual instruction compounded by the students seemingly protecting themselves by watching the class happen rather than engage it.

I let it happen, knowing that many of them were struggling with the online format, the pandemic, family issues such as unemployment and crowded living spaces, their futures put in question as job offerings dried up. There needed to be empathy for their situation. What they were learning in my ethics class seemed diminished in comparison to the larger life lessons taking place.

The experience was exhausting, lecturing to a computer screen when what I wanted was to get the class to engage in discourse. I feed off the energy classrooms, and that energy just didn't transfer to the online format. A few students did regularly share their cameras and voice their opinions. The best moments were when students videotaped presentations and shared those with the class. It was enough to make the online format work. All the students passed the class; I was thankful for that. I was thankful when the term ended, so I could get some mental rest and try to figure out how to fix my online pedagogical woes before classes resume in the fall.

My first inclination is to be as serene as possible in preparation for fall instruction, to enter the academic year deeply serene, and to maintain that for the rest of the year. I'm reminded of a passage from Pirsig:

> Peace of mind isn't at all superficial. ... It's the whole thing. That which produced it is good maintenance; that which disturbs it is poor maintenance. What we call workability of the machine is just an objectification of this peace of mind. The ultimate test's always your own serenity. If you don't have this when you start and maintain it while you're working you're likely to build your personal problems right into the machine itself.

I remind myself of this passage frequently, keep it on a laminated piece of paper in my wallet. This idea that peace of mind is the whole thing, and the whole thing needs daily maintenance. The real-time, ongoing test is your own serenity. My students know when I have peace of mind. They see it in how I teach: if laughter is part of the class dialogue, if I'm honest with them about my own struggles with the course content, if I honestly tell them when I'm mentally struggling and prefacing class by letting them know, "Hey, class may be shorter than normal today, because I'm having a rough day."

I love the classroom, because I've been trained to engender meaningful discourse. I have a detailed syllabus, assignments where students write thoughtful, reflective essays. We meet on a scheduled basis. I get to know most of them by name. It's a wonderful pattern that repeats itself every semester, every academic year for the last thirty-one years.

Maybe this is what hits me in the face about the protests. Most of the people in the marches are the same age as my students. They're placing themselves in harm's way—not just from the police but from the pandemic. The best marches are peaceful and organized. But then curfews hit, the police arrive, and mayhem tends to ensue.

8.

Yesterday was June 4, the anniversary of the 1989 massacre in Tiananmen Square. Public dissent in China began on April 15, but it was suppressed on June 4 when the government declared martial law and sent the military to occupy central Beijing. When I think about the Tiananmen protests, I think of the defining photograph of one man standing in the way of tanks that had been sent to crack down on peaceful student protests.

China is currently pushing for new national security laws that will curtail Hong Kong's ability to be Hong Kong, a capitalistic city that provides its citizens with personal freedoms. Evan visited Hong Kong last summer and told me that he felt safe there, much safer than where he currently lives in Portland. When I was Evan's age, I traveled to Hong Kong to visit a friend who was serving as an English tutor for Vietnamese refugees; she brought me to the compound where the refugees were harbored. They were eager to learn English, to pursue the opportunity to relocate to Canada, a country that accepted Vietnamese refugees. I love Hong Kong, not just what it represents but what it enables its citizens to experience.

Before the protests of the death of George Floyd, it was the Hong Kong Umbrella Revolution. Before that, it was the 2013 protests in Turkey, the 2011 Bahraini uprising, the Indian anti-corruption movement, Ukraine's Orange Revolution, the 2003 Rose Revolution in Georgia. In this country, it's been the Black Lives Matter movement, the Los Angeles Black Cat Protest, draft resistance, the Civil Rights movement, the Chicano movement, women's suffrage, the Cherokee removal. A long history of nonviolent resistance and a long history of violence. I'm reminded of Martin Luther King Jr., of Mahatma Gandhi, leaders we return to when exemplifying cultural acts of peaceful demonstration.

Then I circle back to Pirsig, the concentric circle drawing I discuss with students. Action is an outer ring. Action is preceded by thoughts and values, and at the center is peace of mind. If peaceful demonstration is an act, then it is preceded by the thought of peaceful demonstration, the defined value of peaceful demonstration and, at the core, serenity. If one is serene during nonviolent resistance, then that serenity may be even more evident.

Ethics, by definition, is the branch of philosophy that involves systematizing, defending, and recommending concepts of right and wrong conduct. The whole point about establishing one's ethics, morals, and values is to engage in right conduct. Which begs the question: How does one conduct oneself in such a way as to exercise defined values—whether there's a pandemic or cultural revolution taking place or not.

In the ethics class, I talk about Emanuel Kant, the German philosopher who defined and differentiated *a priori* and *a posteriori* knowledge:

- a priori: knowledge acquired prior to "sense experience"
- a posteriori: knowledge gained from experience

We make lists of examples—things that we've learned *a priori* and what we've learned *a posteriori*. I tell them that my decision to go to graduate school was an *a priori* decision, because I had no experience or knowledge as to what graduate school was like. I didn't know anyone who had attended graduate school, other than a few people who went to seminary, so making the decision to attend grad school, and thus spending the next nine years of my life in grad school, was based on an idea, not on experience. I had the experience of attending high school and college, but they were nothing like graduate school, not by a long shot.

An example of *a posteriori* knowledge would be when I decided to pursue a career as a professor. For years, I taught as a graduate student, and when I completed graduate school I found a job in high tech and worked part time as an instructor at a local college. I knew what teaching and research were; I had those experiences, so it wasn't a big jump to begin a career as a full-time academic.

I think about these different types of knowledge when I think about the difference between nonviolent resistance and violent resistance:

- nonviolent resistance: one would have to go to a protest with the idea of engaging in nonviolent protest
- violent resistance: often the result of acting before thinking about the consequences of those actions, though there are plenty of protesters who protest with violence in mind

I am not a violent person. I think a great deal about how best to treat people: first my wife and children, then my students. Those few times when I have acted violently, those actions were spontaneous, not premeditated. When Kait was in second grade, we were roughhousing in a pool. I would pick her up and throw her into the deep end. Once, unfortunately, I picked her up and she slipped; I sent her face-first into the bottom of the shallow end. She came up with a mouth full of blood and tears. I started to cry too, in disbelief that this had happened, that I was the cause of this accident. I never played with her, or Evan, like that again.

Life is a mix of *a priori* and *a posteriori*. I think philosophers love the idea of *a priori* knowledge because they spend a ton of time thinking before acting.

I value nonviolent resistance because it requires thought. What frightens me about violence is when perpetrators give it premeditated thought.

31

9.

When I started the "Bike to local parks and attempt to sit still until you can no longer do it and then, and only then, begin to write" ritual, I planned on going to a different park every day. Yet today I'm back at the park with a picnic table overlooking Lake Michigan, the expansive view, a setting for distance and perspective. Down below in the lake, dozens of ducks dive for fish as seagulls hover above them. Except for the people conversing as they walk the path behind me, all is relatively still.

I took a few days off from my morning trips to the parks. I had intended to ritualize this activity every day throughout the summer, to give discipline and structure to the process of pondering the topic of serenity. But that's not happening. Instead, I read and process Internet articles on police brutality and cultural racism. They are not topics I typically study, but I want to understand what's culturally happening now and how what's happening connects to my intent to be serene.

Sue and I recently moved into a 1947 Cape Cod house on an acre of land. Across the street is Bob, a neighbor I see maybe once a week. The other neighbor is Barbara, whom we correspond with via notes left in mailboxes—she rarely leaves her house. The other two sides of the property abut a nature preserve: birds, beaver, turkeys, deer, ground hogs, and snapping turtles make their way across the property with regularity. We love this house and the quiet it provides, but it's at odds with the stories Kait and Evan tell me when we talk on the phone. They're in their twenties, and they live near city centers.

I work in downtown Milwaukee, a sixteen-mile bike ride from home. When we first moved up here I commuted, two to three hours a day on the bike depending on weather. I'm committed to biking to work; moving up here grounded the commitment. I want our new country lifestyle to serve as a similar commitment to serenity.

If I spend most of my day cycling on a bike path and living among trees and animals, then the opportunity for serenity increases. I've spent chunks of my adult life living near the outskirts: in a cabin outside Fairbanks; in a double-wide trailer outside Pullman; in a dilapidated house on the edge of the small town of Colton, Washington; on a horse farm outside Coupeville on Whidbey Island. It wasn't until Kait and Evan had to go to school that Sue and I moved near a city, so they could go to good schools and I could be near the university that offered me a job. It only makes sense that, as soon as Kait and Evan left and went to college, Sue and I moved back to the country.

I want to be in a tranquil space that affords tranquil thought. Quiet spaces help quiet the mind.

I like the way I think while riding a bike. Either I engage in what Nishida would call "non-thought," when the mind is active but not focused on anything in particular, or I ponder various topics. When a student tells me they're bored, I tell them I haven't been bored in about thirty years. Not just because I'm in a thirty-year relationship with someone who is a learner, who brings new stories and information home with her every night, but also because I always have a running list of topics in my head that I like to think about.

Before we moved away from the city, it would take me about forty minutes to bike to work and back. Now, when I do go to work, it takes two to three hours, depending on weather, which impacts which bike I ride:

- The Tern: an easy-riding electric-assist bike that I bought for this longer commute, for days when I need to get to work in an hour's time

- The Sequoia: my go-to bikepacking bike I bought for a bikepacking adventure that was supposed to happen this summer, but isn't happening due to the pandemic

- The Wabi: a single-speed bike that's lightweight and ideal for windless days

- The Salsa: my touring bike, now mounted with full fenders, which makes it the go-to ride when there's wet weather

- The Fatboy: a fat-bike with a studded front tire designed for riding in wintry, snowy months

The bike I ride depends on what a given day brings, and the bike impacts the kind of thought I have while cycling. Some bikes require more effort than others and demand that I pay attention to them. The Fatboy, for example, is ridden only when there's snow and ice on the bike path, and that requires focus. The Tern, in contrast, is effortless; it lets me ponder.

Now that it's summer, I'm not commuting to work to teach; and now that we're in a pandemic, it's likely that when classes resume in the fall, I'll continue to teach online, assuming there's another wave of COVID-19. If I'm biking two to three hours a day, then I'm pondering for two to three hours a day, and that enables me to be more me, which is why I'm currently sitting at this picnic table, trying to have a similar thought experience.

I'm interested to see just how sitting still, in the outdoors, is different and similar to how I think on a bicycle. Can I delve deeper into a given line of inquiry because I'm sitting still, not distracted by the stimulation of the ride? Does stillness of body lead to stillness of thought? I'm over a week into this thought experiment, and I'm far from finding answers.

I bike to the parks, look for picnic tables, and sit. The cycling prepares me for sitting still. It's much easier to sit on a bike and ride than it is to sit at a picnic table. Maybe it's because I've been biking my entire life; sitting still isn't part of my history.

I can sit still in my office at work for hours at a time, but I usually do that in response to mental exhaustion, to teaching for several hours at a time, when I need a mental refresh. This thought experiment is different. I'm going into each thought opportunity mentally fresh. I want to sit still, outside, and see what passes for thought.

10.

I'm at the Hubbard Park Beer Garden, watching the Milwaukee River flow by. The garden just opened, and there's a long line of patrons waiting to order beer, pretzels, or brats. I'm content to wait for the line to die down. Few people wear masks; maybe they assume we're safe because we're outdoors.

It's been a good day so far: coffee with Sue, a long dog walk, a breakfast of fresh savory biscuits made from scratch, a bike ride downtown to talk with Mark about Sam Hammill's translation of Basho's *Narrow Road to the Interior*. Mark appreciates Basho's poetry and prose, as well as Hammill's gift at translation. A great conversation.

Then I stopped off at the office on campus and reread Blackburn's *Being Good: A Short Introduction to Ethics*. Blackburn does a good job capturing the reader's attention, helping them understand the value of establishing one's ethical paradigm. In the first chapter he cites Hitler, who said, "How lucky it is for rulers that men cannot think." It's a choice quote when trying to capture a reader's attention, how Hitler thought and his desire to rule those who don't have an active mental life. Blackburn argues that most people are not aware of their own ideas. It sounds somewhat condescending. But it does get the reader's attention.

"Ethics is disturbing," Blackburn writes. It is disturbing that we, as a species, are vaguely uncomfortable when "we think of such things as exploitation of the world's resources, or the way our comforts are provided by the miserable labour conditions of the third world." Or the pandemic and the marches for George Floyd. I'm disturbed by these new cultural and social developments, and I want to find peace of mind, which means spending more time reading books such as Blackburn's, more time sitting on park benches trying to connect ethical ideas to today's cultural confrontations, more time reflecting on my own cultural privilege. I'm sitting in a park, waiting to drink a liter of IPA, trying to enjoy the tranquility of this environment. This setting that I pursue is far removed from protest marches and emergency rooms full of COVID patients.

Evan marched as a form of social protest in Portland. I'm both proud of him and concerned. He told me that he wore a mask, that he left as soon as the protesters started throwing bottles at the police, as soon as the police responded with tear gas. But this is what a son tells his father: not too many details, so I can believe that he's both socially active and safe.

PART TWO

Following the Moral Compass

11.

I'm at a picnic table just off the bike path, a couple blocks from home. It's far enough from the bike path that I'm socially distanced from those riding or walking by, yet close enough to establish eye contact. Some wear masks while biking or running, most don't. It seems the farther you are from the city, the fewer people wear masks and socially distance. My hypothesis is that the more people you see wearing masks and staying six feet apart, the more real the pandemic is. If you know people who have contracted COVID-19, then you're one degree away from the pandemic. It's no longer a news story; it becomes your own narrative.

I know several people who have contracted the virus. I tell them "I'll keep you in my thoughts," a statement I mean with great sincerity. I believe in the power of thought, just as I believe in the power of prayer: focusing attention on something has an effect. I've also found that the more I ruminate on troubling news, such as a friend or family member contracting a life-threatening virus, the more I come to terms with it. Ruminating, not freaking out. Understanding and accepting, rather than ignoring or overreacting.

I'm thinking some more about the Pirsig Paradigm, wondering where one begins if one wants peace of mind. Do you go directly to the center and focus on being serene, or do you begin with your values, define them, and let them work in two directions, toward the center (peace of mind) and outward (thought)? Or do you start with your actions and reverse-engineer your way to serenity?

I know from experience that it helps to reflect and then write about what I value. It's helpful that I require students to define their values. Years ago, I simply asked them to write an essay on their values: where they came from, how they exercise them. But recently, I've asked more of them. Now they're required to document their ethics along with their morals, personal mission statement, and personal vision statement, along with some examples.

As they try to figure out the direction of their moral compass, they eventually ask me what my values, ethics, morals, and personal mission and vision statements are. This requires me to revisit these paradigms every time I teach the class. I'm routinely required to revisit my moral compass and ask myself if it still represents who I am and who I aspire to become. This is what I have as of now, the summer of 2020:

Personal mission in life: Express the Divine.

Personal vision: Maintain the "self" in the pursuit of serenity

And I have the following table of interconnected values, ethics, and morals:

VALUE	MORAL/ETHIC	CONDUCT
Serenity • **Awareness** • **Silence** • **Reflection**	• Let the past and future be the present • Oneliness, Solitude • A = A if A does not = A	• Minimize stimulus, minimize thought • Sit alone whenever possible • Listen more, speak less • Sleep, sleep, sleep
Adventure • **Exploration** • **Family** • **Freedom**	• go off course • controlled risk • Sue, then Kait/Evan	• Commute on a bike • Prepare to tour • Tour—solo and with Sue/Kait/Evan

VALUE	MORAL/ETHIC	CONDUCT
Learning • **Passion** • **Intuition** • **Outdoors**	• What's good for Rush is good for Dave • Be the bikes • Time in the Divine	• Know Rush (this dog knows what I need to know) • Sustained reading/writing/researching • refine mental filters • more time outside than inside

There's a lot to unpack in all this information. I put the table on the projector, my students ask questions, and I try to explain. I tell them that my personal mission in life, my response to the age-old question "What's the meaning of life," is to express the Divine, to be a living representative of what I consider to be God. I tell them that I view nature not as God's creation but as God's manifestation, which is why I long to be outdoors, because I believe that nature is Divine. And when I'm outside, in the presence of rivers and lakes and trees, I am with God.

I tell them that my vision statement—the sentence that captures what I aspire to become—focuses on maintaining the balance needed to actualize serenity. It's right out of Pirsig's quote: that which produces serenity is good maintenance, and that which disturbs it is poor maintenance, but you always have to maintain "the machine," yourself. This resonates with me because for the first four decades of my life, I believed that one could simply arrive at serenity, purpose, and actualization, that it wasn't something you had to maintain every moment of every day. When I did come to that understanding, I felt overwhelmed. But then I began to be intentional about the daily maintenance, and the more I try, the more it becomes normal, and the more I experience the person I envision myself to be.

The mission statement reflects who I am; the vision statement reflects who I aspire to become. Simple short phrases that I keep in my head and revisit when pursuing the serene.

12.

I'm at a picnic table in Freistadt, a small farming town west of the house. Not much to this unincorporated township other than houses, a couple of inns, a church, and an auto shop, which makes it an ideal place to write this morning. The church has a play area where a woman swings her child; that's about it for social activity. It helps that I'm in the shade of six pine trees: the sun's up, and it's going to be a hot day. Best to get my sitting and writing done before the sun is high in the sky.

Sitting in this park is in sync with my personal mission statement to express the Divine. I've never heard God speak to me in English, which is ironic since I spent decades of my life praying for Him to do so. It became much easier to hear the voice of God when I realized that it wasn't going to occur through words. It would have to be through silence, or through what one hears when listening to silence. This morning I hear a woman laughing with her child, the wind pushing maple leaves, and a cardinal singing.

I don't think as much about my vision statement as about my mission statement, probably because I'm not much of a forward-thinking person. Nor am I someone who ponders the past. In fact, I question the "western" classification of past, present, and future and embrace the Buddhistic emphasis on "being present." To be present you focus on the present, especially since the past seems to lead to regret, and the future is nothing but anxiety.

My students are often anxious, in part because they don't know what's going to happen to them when they graduate. Will they find a good job, pay off their student loans, find a suitable life partner, be fulfilled? Lots of questions they can't answer, which creates anxiety. Those are big-picture questions. What they really, really focus on is the near-present: the quiz they have later in the week, the report that's due by the end of the semester. Those things preoccupy their thoughts and prevent them from being aware of what's going on right now.

One of my ethics is "Let the past and future be the present." It tells me that, if I reflect on the past or plan for the future, it needs to be in relation to what's going on right now, because the past and future are not real. Only this moment is. The future is not real. Who knows what's about to happen? If you would have told me four months ago that we'd be in a full-swing pandemic, that I'd be wearing a mask whenever I go out, that I'd only leave the house for the occasional bike ride, I would have had a hard time believing you.

I've read articles on just how long a "moment in time" lasts. Most philosophical scientists say a moment lasts anywhere between five and fifteen seconds. That doesn't seem like much, which is why I like the idea of simply not believing in the past or the future, because that allows the present to stretch on indefinitely and in different directions. What I did yesterday, and what I'll do tomorrow, are what I'm doing now, because there is no yesterday or tomorrow. Yes, the earth orbits the sun, which gives us "night," which is different from "day" and thus provides us with words that give structure to past and future. But it just seems arbitrary. The length of a day on Mars differs from the length of a day on Earth. If Earth were the size of Mars, we'd have a different concept of yesterday and tomorrow.

I hate clocks. The classes I teach last fifty minutes. What happens if we're in the midst of a great discussion, and the fifty-minute class expires? The discussion suddenly ends, as the students pack up and leave the room. I like telling my students that I can predict the future: If we're a half-hour into class, I tell them that in twenty minutes they will all pack up their bags and in unison walk out of the classroom. I tell them I know it will happen because I've seen students do it on a regular, scheduled basis for the last 31 years. It's an established pattern, habituated behavior.

It's important that when I tell my students that "Let the past and the future be the present" is my ethic, they understand that just because it's my ethic, it doesn't need to be theirs. It's not my job to tell them what to believe or do. It is my job to make sure they have guiding principles that give direction to their beliefs and actions. Their job is to create their own ethics, not imitate mine.

I hate being told what to do and believe; I think this is true for most of us. The reason students pursue degrees is that they can learn how to create the person they aspire to be. Their job isn't to memorize facts, it's to make decisions about how they want to behave and then to behave that way. Be the person you aspire to be right now, in this moment. It always sounds so simple when I tell this to them, and they always tell me I'm wrong, that it sounds extremely difficult.

☙

On my way back to the house, I decide to stop at Lempke Park. It's noon, hot, and I need another bike-break. Lempke Park is a group of Little League baseball fields, horseshoe pits, an archery range, picnic areas, and green pasture—very Wisconsin. Though no one is playing here due to the pandemic, the baseball diamonds and surrounding fields are well managed. It would appear that the county continues to employ its groundskeepers.

On my bike ride from Freistadt to here, I thought about another idea I share with my students—not just in the ethics class, but in all classes. The idea is how higher education is about building a bridge between the tangible and the intangible. Serenity, for example, is abstract. It's a concept. I cannot hold serenity in my hands, just as I cannot hold other ideas such as love, solitude, and intuition. What I can hold in my hands are the tangibles: my bike, the water bottle beside me, the laptop I'm typing on. Higher education is about helping students connect the real to the ethereal. Building a bridge, I tell my Mechanical Engineering students, is a tangible activity, because bridges are tangible, but it takes a lot of math to know how to build a bridge, and math is nothing but abstraction. The more complex the math, the more abstract it becomes. The English language is the same: The longer words become, the more abstract they tend to be.

I ask my students what they value. I give them a list of example values and ask them to find five or six that they identify with. I provide them with a list generated by Scott Jeffrey, two hundred different values, and ask them if there are a half-dozen that resonate:

Acceptance	Certainty	Cooperation
Accomplishment	Challenge	Courage
Accountability	Charity	Courtesy
Accuracy	Cleanliness	Creation
Achievement	Clear	Creativity
Adaptability	Clever	Credibility
Alertness	Comfort	Curiosity
Altruism	Commitment	Decisive
Ambition	Common sense	Decisiveness
Amusement	Communication	Dedication
Assertiveness	Community	Dependability
Attentive	Compassion	Determination
Awareness	Competence	Development
Balance	Concentration	Devotion
Beauty	Confidence	Dignity
Boldness	Connection	Discipline
Bravery	Consciousness	Discovery
Brilliance	Consistency	Drive
Calm	Contentment	Effectiveness
Candor	Contribution	Efficiency
Capable	Control	Empathy
Careful	Conviction	Empower

Endurance
Energy
Enjoyment
Enthusiasm
Equality
Ethical
Excellence
Experience
Exploration
Expressive
Fairness
Family
Famous
Fearless
Feelings
Ferocious
Fidelity
Focus
Foresight
Fortitude
Freedom
Friendship
Fun
Generosity
Genius
Giving
Goodness
Grace
Gratitude
Greatness
Growth
Happiness
Hard work
Harmony
Health
Honesty
Honor
Hope
Humility

Humor
Imagination
Improvement
Independence
Individuality
Innovation
Inquisitive
Insightful
Inspiring
Integrity
Intelligence
Intensity
Intuitive
Joy
Justice
Kindness
Knowledge
Lawful
Leadership
Learning
Liberty
Logic
Love
Loyalty
Mastery
Maturity
Meaning
Moderation
Motivation
Openness
Optimism
Order
Organization
Originality
Passion
Patience
Peace
Performance
Persistence

Playfulness
Poise
Potential
Power
Present
Productivity
Professionalism
Prosperity
Purpose
Quality
Realistic
Reason
Recognition
Recreation
Reflective
Respect
Responsibility
Restraint
Results-oriented
Reverence
Rigor
Risk
Satisfaction
Security
Self-reliance
Selfless
Sensitivity
Serenity
Service
Sharing
Significance
Silence
Simplicity
Sincerity
Skill
Skillfulness
Smart
Solitude
Spirit

Spirituality	Temperance	Understanding
Spontaneous	Thankful	Uniqueness
Stability	Thorough	Unity
Status	Thoughtful	Valor
Stewardship	Timeliness	Victory
Strength	Tolerance	Vigor
Structure	Toughness	Vision
Success	Traditional	Vitality
Support	Tranquility	Wealth
Surprise	Transparency	Welcoming
Sustainability	Trust	Winning
Talent	Trustworthy	Wisdom
Teamwork	Truth	

Every one of those values is abstract, unreal, cannot be held in one's hand. But they can be exemplified through one's actions. If I value the concept of silence, then I can enact it by sitting still for as long as possible in a setting that has little stimulation. That's how I exercise silence. And that silence is connected to the experience of serenity, which is again something I value highly, which means I need to continue to find picnic tables in parks where no one else is. If I'm lucky, then I can carry that serenity into environments that are not as low-stimulus.

Not many of my students value serenity. I think it's an idea that they don't often encounter. The environment they live in, academia, is not a suitable setting for exercising peace of mind. Maybe that's why I find it necessary to have this conversation with them. I want students to become good engineers and nurses, good business professionals. I always gravitate toward coworkers who have that sense of serenity, colleagues who can exercise peace of mind in stimulus-rich environments. I don't find them often, which is why I make a point of getting to know them when they are present.

I highly value the students who are good learners, good writers, and good students in general. The best of them have this sense of serenity, whether they're aware of it or not.

13.

It's six in the morning, and I'm having a cup of coffee in a campground at Harrington Beach State Park, about thirteen miles north of the house. I wanted to create an opportunity, a night dedicated to "just sitting," so I put my camping gear on the bike and headed to this campsite. The bike ride getting here was nothing but fun—all tailwind up a bike path and then farming roads. The sun was high in the sky, and the air cooled as I approached Lake Michigan. Setting up camp is always fun, and always simple, since I don't carry much gear with me: you can only bring what you can fit on the bike. Instead of using the bike touring setup, with four paniers and plenty of room to carry whatever you want to bring along, I brought instead the bikepacking bags that I purchased last year. The bags attach to the frame of the bike, so when you're riding, it feels like you're riding a bicycle instead of a bike with four full paniers hanging off it.

I wasn't supposed to be in Milwaukee this summer. I was supposed to be bikepacking. The plan was to ride the Great Divide Mountain Bike route with Evan, from Canada to the Mexican border, up and down the Continental Divide. It was going to be Evan's graduation gift, an opportunity for the two of us to spend a couple of months together and get to know each other again. We canceled the trip because of the pandemic.

The ride to this campsite was simple enough, no different than any other day when I ride a bike. I set up camp and haven't left it, content to sit at the picnic table and enjoy a bottle of cabernet sauvignon.

This overnight bike trip seems to hit my three main values: serenity, adventure, and learning. It's certainly a serene setting, in the Wisconsin woods far enough from other campers, sitting still for hours, listening to red winged blackbirds sing to each other. I'm not too sure if it's adventurous, given that I'm not waking up in the Rockies. You could say that surviving the pandemic is itself an adventure. This is certainly a good place to learn, and I love to learn outdoors. So far on this trip, I've learned how to use the bikepacking setup, how to delay dinner as long as possible so as to enjoy the burrito I bought while biking up here all the more, and, most importantly, I'm continuing to learn the process of ritualistically sitting still. I love riding my bike, how it makes me think, and I've spent countless days of my life pondering on the bike, but I haven't spent much time intentionally sitting still. I'm glad I'm giving it a go, now that I have the summer off, now that the kids are living their own lives and no longer at home, now that Sue's consumed with her veterinary career.

When I say that I value serenity, that I value the outdoors, I should probably explain what I mean by value. When I ask my ethics students to draft their values and ethics, I have to help them understand the relationship between these concepts. Values generally refer to the beliefs a person has, those one-word concepts that are big and abstract. I value "serenity" – but explaining what serenity is takes more than a single word. Ethics, in comparison, are sentences rather than single words, sets of rules that govern the behavior of a person, and typically they're supported by a group or culture that the individual aligns with. If I value serenity, and I want to behave in a serene way, it helps to connect the value to an ethic.

One of my ethics that I enact as a way of exercising serenity is "Oneliness" – a word we don't use anymore. As it is defined by Fay Bound Alberti:

The term "loneliness" first crops up in English around 1800. Before then, the closest word was "oneliness", simply the state of being alone. As with solitude – from the Latin "solus" which meant "alone: – "oneliness" was not coloured by any suggestion of emotional *lack*. Solitude or oneliness was not unhealthy or undesirable, but rather a necessary space for reflection with God, or with one's deepest thoughts. Since God was always nearby, a person was never truly alone. Skip forward a century or two, however, and the use of "loneliness" – burdened with associations of emptiness and the absence of social connection – has well and truly surpassed oneliness.

I found the concept of oneliness when doing research on loneliness. I wanted to read up on loneliness, since I haven't experienced it in a while. I love the history of the word oneliness, how it precedes loneliness, how loneliness came about as a result of the second industrial revolution, when people moved to crowded cities and enacted manufacturing jobs that were not directly related to their lives outside of work, creating products that they probably didn't have at their own disposal. How we moved away from nature when we moved into urban environments. It's one of the ironies I experience with solitude: the more time I spend alone (and outside), the less I feel lonely, to the point where I'm no longer sure I understand what loneliness is.

My lack of loneliness also has to do with my marriage to a smart, funny, functional person, and the time I spend communicating with Kait and Evan—these three people I care most about, my wife and children. That's why I made another ethic for myself: under the value of "Adventure," I follow the rule of "Sue, then Kait/Evan," which means I can't always go on solo bikepacking and bike touring adventures. As much as I'd prefer doing just that, it's important to share the experience with Sue, Kait, and Evan, so my desire for solitude and oneliness don't put those relationships at risk.

I should also differentiate the concept of "ethic" from that of "moral." The terms are related, to the point where some philosophers don't distinguish one from the other. But when my students ask me how the words differ, I tell them that ethics typically derive from the institutions we affiliate with: our faith communities, our social organizations, our employers. Morals are "rules" that we follow separate from the institutions we align with.

Several years ago, a student asked me which institutions I align with, so I made a list on the board, and then, as a class, we googled the mission statement for each institution:

1. The Milwaukee School of Engineering (my employer):
   - **Collaboration** – We value working together across boundaries.
   - **Excellence** – We value the pursuit and achievement of excellence.
   - **Inclusion** – We value authentic engagement with diverse people, beliefs and ideas.
   - **Innovation** – We value creativity and new ideas for lifelong service, discovery and growth.
   - **Integrity** – We value doing the right thing in a reliable way.
   - **Stewardship** – We value the responsible use of our resources.

2. Humanities, Social Science, and Communication (the department I teach in): To ensure that every MSOE graduate is well-rounded through thought-provoking courses that enhance students' studies and lives.

3. Blue Ear Books (my publisher): publishing and disseminating selected new and reprinted nonfiction books of particular global topical or cultural interest.

4. Adventure Cycling (the organization that provides the routes I follow when bike touring): to inspire and empower people to travel by bicycle.

5. Bikepacking.com (the go-to website for bikepackers): to inspire readers to get out and explore our planet, discover its wild places, and connect to its diverse cultures, all via the bicycle's elegant simplicity.

6. Northern Brewer (the company I buy home-brew materials from): To help our fellow homebrewers make great beer.

7. Amazon (the resource I purchase from regularly, especially in this pandemic): to be earth's most customer-centric company; to build a place where people can come to find and discover anything they might want to buy online.

I told the students that examining this list of mission statements truly helps me understand who I am. I value working for a university that values inclusion and innovation. I value bikepacking.com because they place emphasis on discovering wild places.

After this exercise, I had each student make a list of the institutions they align with. I asked them to look up the mission statements of their institutions, then I asked if the language of those mission statements resonated with them or not. The students who knew the institutions they aligned with said, yes, it resonated, and the students who weren't sure which institutions they aligned with just weren't sure. I told them that it's okay if they're not sure, for the simple reason that they are in a place of discovery. They can reflect on which institutions influence them the most, and if they're good with that.

It's not normal to come up with one's defined ethics. I often wonder if anyone does this kind of work outside university classrooms. There are institutions designed to give you ethics, but what institution helps you discover your own? I think the reason the university has me teach "ethics" and not "values" or "morals" is that they want the students to follow the rules set up by them by their given institutions, especially those that employ them. If we follow these definitions, then my "moral compass" is more "morals" than "ethics," because I opt to create my own rules. I doubt you'll find an institution that values oneliness, since oneliness is about solitude, and institutions in general don't actively support solitary activities, since they tend to create and support communities that have common purpose.

I like having defined values, ethics, and morals, because it's really all about "conduct," or what we do. Nishida differentiates "conduct" from "actions" by asserting that conduct is the behaviors we engage in that align with our values. If you don't have a "moral compass," I tell my students, then you have no tool to use to give you direction in life, and it's good to have direction. If they graduate with an engineering degree, they can use it to change the world, for better or worse. I prefer that they change it for the better, so I require them to define their values, ethics, and morals.

14.

This morning I'm at Upper Lake Park in Port Washington, a town twenty miles north of home, overlooking the shores of Lake Michigan. Today is another hot day, and on hot days I opt to sit still near the Great Lake that acts as a grand natural air conditioner.

I've been ruminating this morning about sitting still and my need to give myself permission to sit still. Most of my life, I've been in a rush: get the academic degrees, get the good job, raise the children, try to make a difference. All that hurrying disables one's ability to simply sit still. I had to make it a value if I were ever to hope to learn how to do it. That involves giving myself permission to exercise this behavior every day. No one else was going to give me permission to do this. The culture seems to be in love with busyness, with accomplishing as much as possible.

Last summer, my friend Jay invited me to go sailing in the San Juan Islands in Washington State. Jay's quite successful, working as a vice president for a company that does global supply chain management, moving billions of dollars of product out of China, India, Vietnam—any and all of the countries that create affordable products for American consumers. He lives a stress-filled, busy life, so his yearly vacation involves sailing in the San Juans for two weeks each summer. He invites some friends to join him for the first few days of the trip, then he drops us off and picks up his wife, nephews, and niece. It was good to sail with him, to spend time with him, to catch up on what's happened since we last saw each other.

You would think that sailing is a tranquil, quiet activity, but it's not, at least not in the San Juan Islands. You always check for drifting logs that could potentially crack the hull, check the maps and sonar for rock shallows, check the wind when it's time to turn about as you navigate among the islands. Jay loves all that activity. I don't. I just do what he tells me to do: sync sails, patrol the water with binoculars. And wait for the day's end, when we weigh anchor off some small island, make dinner, and drink.

On the last night of the trip, in the Jones Island harbor, in utter stillness interrupted only by the occasional sea otter, I told Jay that one of my goals in life is to exercise the Japanese concept of *zazen*, sitting still. It's a meditative practice, the primary practice of the Zen Buddhist tradition. Groups of Buddhists sit together in a *zendo*, or meditation hall, bow to their seat, bow to their fellow practitioners, sit on a cushion, ring a bell three times, and sit. I get the ritual of the tradition, the communal and spiritual aspiration. All I want to take away from the practice of *zazen* is the ability to suspend all judgmental thinking and, as Kazuaki Tanahashi would phrase it, to let words and ideas and thoughts pass by without getting involved in them.

Jay's response to *zazen* somewhat surprised me. He said that if everyone's goal was to simply sit still, it would cripple the economy, which doesn't sync with his values, since he loves big business. One of the reasons Jay is a close friend is that we have different values, and we can clearly articulate and defend our values, and we can accept each other despite our value differences. I never expect Jay to value *zazen*, just as he never expects me to pursue the almighty dollar.

I've been emailing with Jay lately to make sure he's okay. He lives on an island outside of Hong Kong, and I worry for him given the political unrest taking place there and how mainland China is imposing its laws on the former British colony. Because of the pandemic, Jay hasn't been able to travel, which is an oddity for him. He's choosing not to leave his little island because of the civil unrest in Hong Kong, so in a way, he's being forced to stay still. Or at least to stay in one place. I need to email him again and ask how he's handling it. He works hard; his brain is always in motion. I'm curious if he spends time looking out over the bay from his front porch, or if he continues to work countless hours, participating in virtual meetings, drafting text messages and emails to his staff.

He's talked about retiring soon, though I'm not sure he'd be good at it. He's worked hard his entire life. Retirement for him would have to involve an activity that would probably require work, something like sailing.

I cannot fault Jay for not making "serenity" an explicit value. Just because I'm pursuing it doesn't mean he should. I'm sure he wouldn't mind being serene; he just isn't designing his life around it.

15.

I'm back at the Hubbard Park Beer Garden, drinking a liter of Central Waters Rift IPA. It's a great beer, extremely hoppy, difficult to drink quickly. A liter of Rift requires you to sit for a bit.

I'm still reflecting on my history with Jay. He travels to Chicago several times a year on business. When he does, he makes a point of driving up to Milwaukee to visit. My kids call him "Uncle Jay" because he is an adopted part of our family. It matters that Jay visits regularly, that he makes a point of talking to my children, asking about how they're doing and what they're up to. He wants to know their ongoing story; he wants to be part of it.

The Japanese have a term, *kenzoku*, which translated literally means "family." It defines the bond between people who are not family but at the same time are. The presence of the deepest connection of friendship, of what Lickerman would describe as "lives lived as comrades from the distant past." Jay knows some aspects of me better than my own wife does; we shared formative experiences together long before I married Sue.

Stanly Sharp defines friends as people you take the time to understand and allow to understand you. Friends like Jay allow me to reserve the term "friend" for those that put an effort into the relationship.

Jay's an old friend. We attended the same high school but went to different colleges. After college, we worked odd jobs, saved our money, and backpacked through Europe. That's when our friendship developed. If you travel with someone, if you share your every moment with them for months at a time, you can learn to become lifelong friends. It wasn't easy traveling with Jay; our friendship was often put to the test, which is why the friendship has survived the test of time.

Jay's always been the smartest person in the room. He's always been well read. When we traveled through Europe, Jay had the habit of pointing out historical markers that we learned about in school, and I would have no idea what he was talking about. When we visited Marrakesh, we walked through Bab Agnaou, a famous gate constructed in 1190, a public entrance to the royal Kasbah. He told me all about it, had the historical details locked into his head, available for real-time recollection. He told me we had both learned about it in Mrs. Wilson's eleventh-grade history class. He'd learned about it. I, on the other hand, hadn't, which made me begin to wonder why.

At one point in the trip, we decided to separate for a couple of weeks so he could visit French cathedrals while I surfed St. Jean de Luz. I thought he was a bit of a nut for visiting historical ruins when he could be riding a long board.

It was fun surfing in France, and I'm sure Jay enjoyed touring cathedrals. I just wish I had come across his type of historical enjoyment earlier in life. You cannot manage who you were, only who you are as a way of managing who you are becoming. I don't think it's healthy to wish things could have been different. You can only manage the "now" really, all we can control is our thoughts.

My desire to become an academic was in large part Jay's influence. I wanted to be able to see the subtext in a situation, to be able to read a room and understand more than what was on the surface. My life at that time was rather literal, and I was tired of seeing the world through that lens. I knew enough about Jay to understand that he was using a different set of lenses.

After we traveled through Europe, Jay went to the University of Chicago to get a doctorate in Chinese history. He didn't have a good experience. Like Pirsig, who also pursued a terminal degree at the University of Chicago, Jay struggled academically, which was new to him. After the first year, his advisor suggested he take some time off, live in a country where they spoke Chinese and dive into the language, then return to the program. Jay chose Taipei and taught English, landed a side job in supply chain management, worked his ass off, and decades later became a vice president for the likes of Coach, Sears, and JC Penny. His story is one of struggle and success, but one that involved ongoing and constant learning. Take chances, make mistakes, work hard, learn, move forward.

Academically, I was fortunate in comparison because there was no way I was going to get into a school as rigorous as the University of Chicago. I was lucky enough to be accepted to the University of Alaska, Fairbanks. I received a great education there, no doubt, but it wasn't Chicago. It was a good program for me because I was still learning how to learn, still had a long way to go before I could be academically competent. In retrospect, it's evident that the three years I spent in Alaska were a bit of a sweet spot in terms of serenity. I was being intellectually challenged, but not to the point where, like Jay, it was breaking me. I wasn't the smartest person in the room, so no one expected me to be intellectual. The Internet wasn't a thing yet, and I couldn't afford a television set, so all I had was a laptop that was barely powerful enough to do word processing.

I wish technology could have plateaued back then, in the early 1990s. A computer was a huge upgrade from a typewriter, but it wasn't a tool for accessing the Internet. I had to go to the library and request books and articles and wait weeks for them to arrive. There was a sense of anticipation. Now, I buy a book on Amazon and it arrives the next day. I love instant gratification, but I miss the waiting, the longing to read a book I was hungry to learn from.

After Alaska, Sue and I moved to eastern Washington so she could attend veterinary school. After Alaska, the Internet arrived. I enjoy this beer garden because there is no wi-fi. I can't afford unlimited mobile data, so right now I'm writing free of the internet's distractions, which allows me to think in a way that opens the door to better-regulated thought. I don't have to react to data; I can sit still, write a sentence, enjoy the beer, look out at the Milwaukee River as it flows by, and write another sentence.

This is the kind of learning experience I wish for my students.

I value the Internet because it enables me to communicate quickly with Jay, even though he lives on the other side of the planet. But it takes ongoing discipline to not tap into it continually for any and all streaming information. Managing all that data is not that different than managing one's own thought process: you have to know when, and how, to shut it off.

Let me revisit the Pirsig quote: "Peace of mind produces right values, right values produce right thoughts. Right thoughts produce right actions and right actions produce work which will be a material reflection for others to see of the serenity at the center of it all." Right thought happens only if you value right thought, which is why I've designed a moral compass (values, thoughts, and morals) that steers me toward "right thought." Right thought means time like this, the beer garden, the river, the surrounding trees, writing, and no Internet, no social media, not even anyone to talk to. Right now, I'm serene by design, with great intent. I like the way I'm thinking right now. If these sentences are any good, it's the result of this place at this time and the way my brain is working in this moment.

16.

I'm not at a picnic table this afternoon. Instead I'm enjoying patio furniture at Libby Montana, a bar a half mile from home. I left the house with the usual intent of cycling to a park, finding a picnic table, sitting for an hour, then writing when inspiration presented itself. But it's noon, and the bar serves the Big Sky Burger, a half-pound of beef topped with Wisconsin cheese curds and caramelized onion gravy. Sue called; she'll join me in a half hour. So there's a window of time to write some thoughts down.

Lately I've been thinking about thinking. I value my education and career, the thought processes it enables. But higher education doesn't promote serenity. I teach a plethora of classes: ethics, creative nonfiction, research methodology, technical writing. I've taught twenty-six different classes over the last sixteen years. It's good to teach new courses; it's the ultimate learning experience. You enter the class and tell the students that you've never taught the class before and have little idea what you're doing, and that you will all have to figure it out together over the course of the semester. At least this is my approach. It's one I enjoy, one that enables everyone in the room to be a learner and disables the typical paradigm of "the sage on the stage."

But thinking like an academic is exhausting, and by the end of the academic school year, I'm mentally shot and ready for a few months to recover. At least that's the idea, an idea I struggle to implement, because it's difficult to stop thinking like an academic when that's the way you always think.

It's a big reason I long for serenity. To find peace of mind, one needs to think in a certain way, a way that's not logical and academic. In my early twenties, I found books on Zen Buddhism. I thought that if I understood the concepts driving Zen, I'd be able to become a practitioner. Jay and I would go to Goodwill to purchase books. I found several texts authored by D. T. Suzuki, one of the first Japanese authors to write about Zen in English. I studied his essays the way I'd been trained to study philosophical texts, marking passages and writing notes in the margins. Here's one quote that's marked in what's now faded yellow highlighter: "Man is a thinking reed but his great works are done when he is not calculating and thinking. 'Childlikeness' has to be restored with long years of training in the art of self-forgetfulness." If only I had had the ability, when I first read those sentences, to put the book down and realize that it's great to read essays on Buddhism, but it would have been better to actually try Zen: to engage in the practice of "just sitting," of not trying to make logical sense of it. Maybe it's easier to study something than it is to practice it.

I studied poetry at that time in my life and went on to get a Master of Fine Arts in Poetry, the focus of my studies in Alaska. I loved reading poets such as William Stafford and James Wright, poets who had a sense of perspective, a strong male voice. I wanted that voice and perspective; I wanted to acquire the wisdom I found in their poems. So many of their poems were from the perspective of a person sitting still, observing what's going on around them. What I didn't understand was that the best way to exercise a mature male voice is simply to sit still and listen.

I wasn't very self-aware then, didn't know who I was, and as a result was not comfortable sitting still, sitting alone. It's an activity I still struggle with, though it's certainly easier to do now than it was then. In my early twenties I didn't "long to be serene." I just wanted to write a good poem. What I didn't know was that the poem I longed to write would only come from separating myself from myself, something that can take place when sitting still.

17.

I'm back at the Hubbard Park Beer Garden, having a liter of Hacker-Pschorr Weisse and a brat. It's humid, sunny, and hot, making the beer all the more refreshing. It's been a week since I've written. I haven't pursued peace of mind as of late, and it doesn't make sense to try to write about serenity when I'm far from serene.

I've been waking up at two in the morning and staring at the ceiling for hours. This is typical behavior, especially when I'm teaching, when thinking about students and curriculum. But now it's summer, and I'm not teaching, and there's nothing to really think about in the middle of the night, other than how I feel anything but serene. Then I have the recurring realization that to be serene involves not thinking so much – which is difficult when you spend your entire adult life learning how to think.

I know there are different ways to think, different paces of thought. And I know how much mental discipline it takes to be able to think fast, then slow.

I used to read and write poetry every day, not knowing then that one of the reasons I was doing it was to slow my brain down. I tell my students that a benefit to reading literature is that it makes you stop and think, that the layered content provided in a "work of literature" forces you to ponder, and that pondering is a skill and a great reason to read literature. I'll tell them that my personal definition of literature is "text that speaks to the human condition."

If we want to learn what it is to be human, and if we want to let art be a vehicle for understanding humanity, then books are a great medium. Unlike other mediums such as painting or sculpting, you can actually carry a book around with you. I always have one or two books with me. This morning, it's Basho's *Narrow Road to the Interior* and Pigliucci's *How to be a Stoic*. One work of literature, one work of philosophical theory. Books that you cannot read quickly, books that slow you down.

I've been thinking about some poems that have always been deep within me. One is by James Wright, *Lying in a Hammock at William Duffy's Farm in Pine Island, Minnesota*:

> Over my head, I see the bronze butterfly,
> Asleep on the black trunk,
> Blowing like a leaf in green shadow.
> Down the ravine behind the empty house,
> The cowbells follow one another
> Into the distances of the afternoon.
> To my right,
> In a field of sunlight between two pines,
> The droppings of last year's horses
> Blaze up into golden stones.
> I lean back, as the evening darkens and comes on.
> A chicken hawk floats over, looking for home.
> I have wasted my life.

It's one of Wright's most controversial poems. the critics argue the final line: "I have wasted my life." Is one's life wasted if one gives an afternoon to observing butterflies, listening to cowbells, watching a chicken hawk float overhead? I love the final line. If this is a wasted life, then let life be wasted. When I'm hyper-vigilantly productive, focused on making a contribution, when I'm burning out because I'm not sleeping well, thought running out of control in the middle of the night, I should reflect on this poem.

Do we all have to contribute so much? Do we have to work so

hard? Our culture values hard workers. My father taught me that one's worth is found in how hard one works. Yet I long to waste time.

Another poem I've committed to memory is Robert Bly's *Driving to Town Late to Mail a Letter*:

It is a cold and snowy night. The main street is deserted.
The only things moving are swirls of snow.
As I lift the mailbox door, I feel its cold iron.
There is a privacy I love in this snowy night.
Driving around, I will waste more time.

Bly's short poem also honors wasted time. The poet is alone. I imagine him in an old pickup truck, in Minnesota, where he lived on a farm. The first three lines of the poem prepare the reader for what Bly calls the "leap statement," the line that introduces the abstract concept that's grounded in the poem's tangible details. In this poem, the poet leaps to privacy, but not just any kind of privacy—the privacy one finds in snow, at night, in rural Minnesota. How does Bly end this tiny poem? By telling us that he will continue to waste time. He celebrates wasted time.

When I reflect on serenity, I think of Wright and Bly. They give poetic voice to "peace of mind." Wright lies in a hammock, and Bly, his lifelong friend, drives alone on a snowy night. Alone, but not lonely, wasting time.

Another quality that draws me to these poems is the single voice of the poet. When you read poems, there's rarely more than one character. Fiction, drama, creative nonfiction—the drama in those genres is typically found in human-to-human interaction. I'm always on the lookout for works of fiction where there's only one character, the protagonist. Two that stand out are Hemingway's short story "Big Two Hearted River" and Pam Houston's "A Blizzard Under Blue Sky." You don't see it often; it's not the kind of drama that readers typically identify with.

That might be one of the reasons poetry is on the decline in our culture. The voice of the single poet doesn't resonate with a general audience. I'm sure it's a big reason I was initially drawn to the medium: short works that captured an emotion that did not revolve around human miscommunication. Almost all human drama stems from miscommunication. If, in a poem, there is only the prerogative of the poet, then the poet speaks to the self, finds audience in the self. That's what I wanted when I learned how to write poems back in the day: to communicate with myself and acknowledge the drama going on around me that had nothing to do with other people.

I can't rely on others to be serene, to pursue peace of mind. I can do this myself and let them know that I'm longing for it, if for no other reason than to explain to them why I want to be alone so much. It's so much easier to be serene in solitude.

Poets such as Wright, Bly, Stafford, Oliver, Hammill, Nye, and Gilbert represent to me a cadre of poets who have captured serenity in verse form. When I look at the shelves of poetry books in my office, I see a collection that I've read for decades. I read them so they could help me find my own poetic voice.

I'm realizing that the process of finding inner poetic voice, that voice that honors silence and serenity, doesn't take place in the pursuit of other serene poetic voices. They serve as examples, but to find my own voice I need simply to sit still and listen.

18.

I'm at Kletch Park. Like so many of the parks I frequent, it borders the Milwaukee River. Today's picnic table is in the shade of a maple at the edge of a grove of tall maples, surrounding an empty soccer field. Again, I'm alone. There are over twenty picnic tables scattered about, but no one else is here on a Thursday morning. Everyone is at work, or on vacation, or riding out the pandemic at home.

COVID research is suggesting that the virus is less likely to spread if you're outside. It isn't the protesters marching for Black Lives Matter that are spreading the virus; it's young people going to clubs. How ironic: it's safer to march outdoors for civil liberties, to march in the shadow of the police, than it is to party in a nightclub.

I feel safe, this exercise in extreme social distancing, the only person in a green field surrounded by green maples. Is it a false sense of security? Am I not living in a pandemic? Yes, but I'm not always at risk. Wear a mask and keep your distance. It's not that hard, at least not for me.

What is becoming difficult is being around anyone. It's been months since I've worked physically around people. Now that work is exclusively virtual, I find myself spending most of the day alone. I thoroughly enjoy deep dives into isolation, but it's beginning to come at a price: it's becoming increasingly difficult to be around others.

Sue comes home from work, and I find myself doing tasks that require one person to work alone. It's work I could have done before she came home, but I wait until she's there. It's not good for the relationship; it lacks balance. I've known for a long time that being alone is good if it prepares me to be with Sue, just as being with Sue is good preparation for being alone. But I must get back to that balance and not overly indulge myself in solitude, not if I want the marriage to work the way it's always worked.

Buddhists and Stoics value the middle path, the avoidance of extremes. I'm finally teaching myself not to work too hard by not working too hard. After decades of working hard, it feels right to waste more time. I need to consciously, or intuitively, find similar balance between marriage and solitude.

I've always told people that I don't understand retirement, probably because I've enjoyed working too much. Work, for me, is teaching, and teaching isn't work per se. I go into a classroom and start a conversation. I try to figure out what it is the students already know and build on that, a process that requires dialogue. Being ready to enter a classroom requires the energy to interact, the kind of energy I derive from solitude. My marriage similarly works when it works this way.

Classes will begin again in a couple of months, but they won't take place in classrooms. They'll be online, which will make it more difficult to engender discourse. It's going to take some deep thought to solve that problem.

I'm grateful I'm not in a long-distance relationship with Sue. The only time we go long-distance is when I'm on a bike tour. I have to give Sue a ton of quality time before heading off on a tour. It's easy to spend a ton of time with her when the tours reach completion.

Maybe this is what retirement will look like: an older, wiser, seasoned version of myself, sitting alone on a park bench. Maybe Sue will be sitting with me; maybe I'll be sitting alone.

The economy is in a recession, and my retirement investments are tanking. I doesn't cost much to ride a bike to a park, sit at a picnic table, and watch the river go by. Maybe this is what I will be able to afford to do; maybe it's good that I'm learning to find pleasure in it.

I chose an academic career because it's cerebral. It requires knowing how to sit still and think, how to read and write for extended periods, how to convince students that these are skills worth engendering. I'm grateful that, as a professor, I don't have to attend strings of meetings. That was the one thing that made me hate my prior career in high tech. I worked with smart people, and that was fun. I just didn't want to be around them all the time.

Twenty years ago, my children played soccer on the field I'm now sitting beside. I remember driving them to soccer games, taking them on bike rides, camping trips, then going home and finding solace in work, since work often required being alone. That was the balance then: be a good father, be a good employee, and find the middle path between those two commitments.

If I could do it all over again, I'd try to find more time to be alone, even just half an hour per day. But when you have a long list of things you need to get done, it's hard to justify stillness. Maybe that's why I want to be alone so much now: to make up for lost time.

I work in a knowledge economy. My profession revolves around helping young people prepare for their entry into the knowledge economy. I paid for college by driving a delivery truck, working a forklift, landscaping. I didn't enjoy the work, but I did enjoy the end of the day, when I had the mental energy to read and write. Now that I read and write for a living, it's difficult to read and write for myself at the end of the day. It's another reason I'm enjoying this summer of cycling to picnic tables. It's why I don't ever want to go back to working too hard.

19.

I'm at the Mequon Nature Preserve, several square miles of restored natural habitat. The preserve is laced with paths through meadows, marshes, clumps of forest. I came here today with the intent of reflecting on "nature" and "the Divine." If my personal mission statement is to "express the Divine," then I should be able to explain why it is that I find divinity outdoors.

The picnic table I'm enjoying this morning is at the end of a narrow path that's at the end of a gravel road. Visitors rarely sit here, given its distance from everything else. Though its secluded, I'm far from alone: I count seven different bird songs. Butterflies and white-winged moths flutter about. Sun and shadows contrast through gusted maple leaves.

I grew up going to church, but I never felt the presence of the Divine there. As a child, I listened to Pastor Roti every Sunday morning service. I'm sure he was a good man, but the sermons were boring, especially for a boy who just wanted to go home and play. As I raised Kait and Evan, we spent Sunday mornings going on bike rides. Every couple of years, they'd ask why we don't go to church, since their friends went to church. I told them that cycling was sanctuary.

I don't think they understood what I was talking about, though I believe they do now. Kait sampled various churches when she was in college and attended a local Unitarian church for several years.

They were the church in her small town that accepted and supported her being gay. When we would visit, she'd take us to church. It was good to meet Kait's faith community, the people who accepted Kait for the wonderful person she is.

Evan is a theater major, and he spent last summer going to a variety of churches to research the lead role he had in a college play, as a minister. He took the time to interview various pastors and attend their services, letting them know he was researching his character. He read the Bible from beginning to end. The pastors were open to Evan's conversations and questions. I'm glad he had that experience.

There was a time in my life when I studied theology. I learned enough to not go too far down that path. The gravel road I biked down an hour ago, the one that brought me to this picnic table, in this nature preserve, is a good metaphor for the path I now pursue. It is worship, no doubt, to sit as still as possible in this space. But it's a far cry from the church environment I was raised in. The sanctuary in the small church I grew up in was considered holy ground. My family would all sit together, taking up an entire pew. I remember listening to my father and older brothers sing hymns and doxology. It was good to worship as a family. It was the time when our family shared common purpose.

Yet I am still a bit bitter about growing up in the church, and it's not good to be bitter about one's upbringing. I've worked at letting go of the resentment I harbor about childhood church experiences. Sunday school and the weekly service on Sunday mornings, the Sunday evening service, Tuesday night Boy Scouts (which met in the basement of the church), a Wednesday evening service—it was a lot of church. It taught me the benefit of spiritual community, having friends share Bible class and youth group activities. In winter, the church would sponsor a ski bus so we could all head to the mountains and enjoy the slopes. My favorite week of summer was

Vacation Bible School, where we memorized Bible verses together. I had two friend groups, one at elementary school and one at church. The friendships at church went deeper.

I attended church religiously until I went to college. I opted to go to a university in Southern California, where no one knew me. I didn't know it then, but I was looking for re-creation, the ability to be someone new. When they were handing out student identification cards, the gal taking my information asked, "Is your name Vern?" I was wearing an orange bowling shirt I had bought at Goodwill, with a name patch that read "Vern." I said, "Yes, I'm Vern." So my college student ID had Vern Howell written on it, and throughout college I was known as Vern.

Vern attended a Southern Californian megachurch. The sanctuary held thousands of people. I enjoyed the anonymity provided in such a grand space. The college students I attended with would go to church on their way to Huntington Beach, where we would surf. After a few months, we just ended up heading to Huntington.

It was odd returning home for Thanksgiving and Christmas break, where family and friends knew me as Dave. There was a bit of a schism going on between Dave and Vern; who I was depended on who I was with.

After a year and a half, I transferred to a university not far from my home in Seattle. I missed my high school and church friends and wanted to reconnect. But the change had been made, and after a few months I realized I was no longer part of my old communities. The person they knew no longer existed and, like many college students, I was no longer exactly sure who I was.

I transferred not long after to a third college, and it was there that I fell in love with reading and writing. Instead of developing a wide friend network, as I'd done in the past, I kept to the English Department, finding comfort in mingling with students who read the same books I was reading. I shifted from extraversion to introversion, from Vern to a new version of Dave: someone more interested in developing a social network with protagonists and literary foils.

After college, I backpacked through Europe with Jay, effectively living outdoors for half a year. After that, I backpacked through Asia, spending most of my time hiking through Nepal and Thailand. And after that I moved to Alaska to pursue a graduate degree—the final frontier, where "outdoors" was everything west, north, and east of Fairbanks. The land of the midnight sun and the aurora borealis. It's no wonder my sense of the Divine morphed to worshiping outdoors.

And after Fairbanks, I pursued another graduate degree, the one that introduced me to Nishida, who wrote that "there is no self in nature," no separation between the subject (in this case, me) and the object (the Mequon Nature Preserve). The more I sit still, the longer I learn to sit still, the less I think about myself, the more I become part of this place, and the more I experience, and express, the Divine. It's simple: find a place to sit still outside and sit still for as long as possible and find yourself in the Divine. Nishida wrote that, in nature, "phenomena lose all of their special characteristics and significance; human beings are no different from clods of dirt." I'm no different than a clod of dirt. Yes, as a human I have characteristics that make me, us, unique as a species—an overly developed cortex, the ability to think in abstraction, to communicate through a complex written symbol system, to stand upright and hold tools with opposable thumbs. We live and work in communities, form families, often mate for life. We are unique, but at the same time we're not different from a clod of earth. If we saw this for what it is, we as a species might take better care of our planet. The more I sit still, the more relevant ecology becomes to me, the greater the connection I find between ecology and theology.

I still value the church. It's one of the few institutions that offer people moral guidance and support. Most of my students turn to scripture for direction; most of them are deeply influenced by their faith communities. I know the Bible provides them with moral direction, and that moral behavior is easier if you surround yourself with others who share your beliefs and behaviors. I just don't sync with it, because I cannot wrap my head around the idea that my soul is separate from the souls of others, or that only humans have souls.

I don't consider myself a Buddhist or a Taoist, but I do agree with a lot of the ideas that stem from these world religions. Of course, formal Buddhism, like Christianity, can be ritualistic and dogmatic, which is part of the reason I choose to experience the Divine in a nature preserve rather than in a temple. I would rather learn how to sit still, to meditate, to lose my self in the shade of a maple tree.

20.

I'm back at Vermond Park, once again overlooking Lake Michigan. It's a hot, humid Sunday morning. The temps are ten degrees cooler here compared to home, and it's still hot. There's no wind, no movement on the water. The park's crowded, probably because it's the Fourth of July weekend. A woman is on her phone, Facetiming with her children, telling them she'll be home soon. A father plays catch with his son. A couple set up hammocks between the trees that edge the cliff. Surprisingly, I'm not bothered by my neighboring parkgoers, which is odd, because usually I'm bothered when I go to a place that's usually abandoned but is not.

I'm weeks into this thought experiment, the daily bike rides to different parks and picnic tables. The routine is having an effect, the habituated behavior of cycling and sitting. I notice it when I'm at home – when, for example, Sue interrupts me while I'm trying to work. This is a typical source of irritation, and I typically try my best to mask my angst so I can listen to what she's trying to tell me. I haven't experienced the irritation in a while. I find myself focusing on breath, what a friend, a yoga instructor, calls "slow and low," breathing slowly from the bottom of the diaphragm. I find myself listening better, and when we're done conversing, I go back to work without the sense of having been distracted. It sounds like a small detail, but it has been historically huge. If I continue to learn from sitting still, learn from spending more time outside, if I can bring that back to domestic life and behave how I behave here, then I may become a better partner for Sue.

It's one thing to experience peace of mind when sitting still, alone, on a bench overlooking Lake Michigan. I'll sit at a picnic table but not facing it; today I'm facing the lake. I'll sit like this until my mind gives in to this place, remaining in that mental space as long as possible. Then I'll turn around, turn on the laptop, and write thoughts down. It's as if non-thinking makes the brain want to think all the more.

Home is different. We're indoors all the time thanks to the pandemic, the July heat, and the Midwestern humidity. Sue thinks of ways to improve our property: weeding, shoveling wood shavings, mowing, fixing the garage. The list seems endless, especially since we purchased a house that has "character." But her desire to fix it up doesn't bother me as much. The "bother" isn't gone; I still feel the irritation, the knowing that this type of work that I'm not fond of, but should learn to become fond of, is going to be an ongoing constant. At least it will be this way until winter, when weeds and grass stop growing, when it's too cold outside to work on the property.

Though I must admit that yardwork is making our marriage better. After thirty years of marriage you get locked into lifestyle and communication patterns. It's good to revise what you do, how you think, how you share yourself. I've known for a long time that the only way to make the marriage better is to make myself better. Cycling and sitting on a routine basis seems to be making me better, but cycling and sitting come easily in comparison to weeding. So much of this has to do with the Buddhistic notion of egolessness, losing one's self to one's activities and surroundings. The more egotistical I am, the worse of a life partner I am. My focus is more on what my needs are rather than the needs of the relationship, which is ironic since the relationship is what I need.

We have company this week. Kait and her partner Sophie drove down from Minnesota to stay with us. I love spending time with them, but historically it's been difficult to share my space, especially in our new home, a place I consider a bit of a sanctuary from reality. The pandemic has fueled the longing to "just stay home," just stay still. I've enjoyed our first day with them, having dinner and beers, playing corn hole, going for a morning dog walk and bike ride. I have a history of enjoying guests for about twenty hours, and then I get irritated and look for ways to hide. I'll tell them I need to take a nap, or to go to the grocery for dinner supplies, or to do some work. Any polite excuse. It will be interesting to see if I fall back into that pattern, or if these bike rides to local parks will change the way I act as a host.

Egolessness. It's such an odd concept. We are such an ego-driven society. It's illustrated by the way we're reacting to the pandemic. People cannot seem to stay away from the beaches, cannot understand that wearing a face mask is a way to protect yourself as well as others. Social distancing seems beyond societal grasp. European countries are starting to open up again, and they're not inviting anyone from the United States into European Union countries.

Learning to sit still, to enjoy one's own company, seems to be a skill we all need to learn right about now. If we could go back to sitting still and staying at home, like we did at the beginning of the pandemic, we could end it. We would overcome the pandemic, and we'd be able to safely and sanely go back to our hectic social lives. Reporters go to resorts and ask beachgoers why they flock to crowded vacation spots, and everyone seems to say the same thing: We're bored, we're experiencing pandemic fatigue.

I've always thought of boredom as an inability to enjoy one's own company. Is it egocentric to say that I enjoy my own company, often to the exclusion of others? Enjoying my own company feels more like an act of egolessness. I think more about myself when I'm with others. The more I can learn to be free of ego, the more I enjoy solitude, the more I get confused by the very concept of boredom.

21.

I'm back at Harrington Beach State Park, this time in a campsite with the family: Sue, Kait, and Sophie. Camping with others is different than camping alone. The three of them biked up here, while I drove the car with all the car camping equipment: tents, sleeping bags and pads, pillows, camp chairs, food for a week. I even brought a cornhole set. The last time I was here, all I had was my tent, sleeping bag, and food for a day, what would fit on my bike. My luxury item was instant coffee for the morning. This time, I brought a six-pack of homemade beer, a three-liter Bota Box of Shiraz, cherries and chips, a dozen burritos we made last night. It's good to have food in a campsite, good to have family to share it with. Yet I'm also reminded just how good it was to be here alone.

We talked and drank beer for several hours after swimming in Lake Michigan. Now everyone's reading books, waiting for dinner time. The last time I was here, I just sat still at the picnic table. Everyone is sitting still now, but sitting in the company of others is different.

It reminds me why I enjoy reading about Zen Buddhism and practicing many of its tenets, yet have no interest in attending a Buddhist shrine or temple, no desire to become part of a Buddhist community. I want to be alone with my spirituality, to enjoy the outdoors by myself, just me and the Divine.

I watch YouTube videos of people who live at Buddhist monasteries. Though the lifestyle appears purposeful, it also looks regimented.

You wake at a specific time, pray at a specific time, clean at a specific time. Even your personal time is designated and scheduled. All that order, the attention to the schedule, doesn't fit my spiritual sensibility. I cannot imagine the Divine operating on a schedule.

I'm sure the monastic life works for those who live in monasteries. Otherwise, why would you choose that lifestyle? I do admire the focus on living with minimal possessions, since possessions can be a distraction.

Not wanting to be part of a monastery, to practice with others, probably goes back to childhood and growing up in the church. I was always told what to do and believe. Which is why, as an adult, I don't like being told what to do, especially when it comes to how to exercise faith.

If everyone at a monastery (or church, or synagogue, or temple) was serene, then I would be attracted to living a religious life and plugging into a faith community. But spiritual institutions seem to have all the trappings of other institutions: the need to pay bills, establish hierarchies, follow dogmas. Sitting still, outdoors, just seems so immediate and accessible. It seems the most uncomplicated way to find the Divine as well as heightened levels of serenity.

My family has its own institutional trappings. We wake up at a specific time, follow the day's routine, do what needs to be done. A benefit to being at this campsite, away from the house and the patterns that exist in domestic life, is that it's different. There are no pets to feed or walk, no floor to vacuum or dishes to clean. Right now, everyone's just doing what they want to do—read. And when we get hungry, we'll eat burritos and drink boxed wine. We'll probably make a fire and strike up a conversation and watch the stars come out before going to sleep. But I'm just speculating; these are the things we typically do when camping, and the beauty of camping, of being away from the patterns of domestic life, is that you can follow a different pattern.

Maybe that's what I'm enjoying about this serenity thought experiment: it introduces new patterns. I leave the house to ride a bike to a park where I can sit, reflect, and eventually write down some ideas about the thought experiment. I like this alteration to the pattern, if for no other reason than that it provides perspective, the ability to see the established patterns I abide by.

PART THREE

Egolessness is Paradoxical

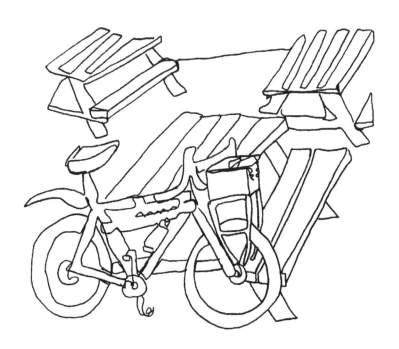

22.

A week's gone by. I haven't been cycling to parks to reflect and write, a pattern disrupted by hosting Kait and Sophie at home. No regrets, though. I love Kait, and I love seeing Kait with Sophie, because they are good for each other, help each other do what they need to do. I'm very, very happy that Kait chose a functional partner to be with. Kait can be moody, as I can be moody, and Sophie seems to even her out.

I'm sitting again in the Thiensville Town Park, just two miles from home. Thunderstorms rolled through last night, dropping over an inch of rain, which crested the river before me. There's good park-drama going on. Two elderly men fish on the river's edge, casting out and walking along the river at the river's pace. An old woman walks her ageing dog so slowly that I can't make out if the dog is walking at her pace or if she's walking at the dog's pace. Behind me the playground, which was closed the last time I was here, is filled with boisterous children. Their mothers sit on a bench and chat.

The more I sit in these parks, the more I see things. Patterns emerge. The established pattern of behaving as if we were not all living in a pandemic is here. The mothers on the benches are not social distancing. No one wears a mask. Everyone probably feels safe because we're outdoors, but it seems like a false sense of security. Last week, a farmers' market took place in this park; I was on a bike ride with Kait and Sophie, and we decided to stop so they could shop for a gift for a friend that's dog-sitting for them. We put our masks on and checked out the produce and baked goods for sale. No one wore a mask. No one exercised distancing. It's as if the lack of responsible behavior were normal. And it makes me a bit cynical. Doesn't everyone else have access to the same media sources I have access to? Don't we all know that these changes in our communal behavior could help minimize the collective pandemic risk?

When I ask myself why no one practices good protocols, a number of reasons come to mind. People don't like being told what to do, just as I don't like being told what to do. But that seems like a weak argument since changing the way we behave while in community could actually save the lives of those in the community. Not believing the pandemic is real could be another reason why folks don't abide by the new social guidelines. After all, you can't see the virus. How can something be real if you can't see it?

But the biggest reason, I think, is habituated behavior. Folks are just in the habit of living life a certain way. You live according to the patterns you establish, and it's extremely difficult to break the patterns. Usually, it requires an outside force: you lose your job, your spouse leaves you, someone you love falls ill. Those major life changes bring about forced change, and people don't generally like change.

I'm not a big fan of change. Every year for the last thirty years, Sue and I have looked at each other and said: "Maybe this year will be different. Maybe life will settle a bit." But things would always happen, and we would always need to change. One year, Evan was hit by a car. The year following, Kait attempted suicide. The year after that, I took a new job at work, and the year after that, I took on a new side-job to help save for Kait's college. Sue's work constantly changes, not just because the science of veterinary medicine is always in flux, but because she transitioned from traditional to holistic medicine. That made for a big shift not only in how she practiced, but in how she viewed her profession as well as herself. It meant changing the way we ate at home, changing the products we use to clean the house, changing the restaurants we frequent. Kait went to college. Evan went to college. We all continued to grow as a result of all the change. We moved forward. We learned to accept that change is a constant. But wouldn't it be nice if things just calmed down for a bit and stayed the same?

In my ethics class, I'll ask the students why people do bad things. We come up with a list: ignorance, poor modeling, greed, being so busy that you don't see what's going on around you, a lack of self-love, narcissism. We talk about all these things and use examples to illustrate them. The students want to talk about what happens in the news, but I insist that we use examples from our own lives. I want the examples to be in close proximity to our real-time behavior. I keep reminding them that we have ethics, our guiding principles, so we can improve our conduct. It's all about conduct: what we do, how we treat people and our surroundings. If it's a given that we're going to change, then let's change for the better.

When we finish the list of why people do bad things, I always tack on "habituated behavior." It's not obvious to the students that this should be on the list; I put it on as a way of forcing the issue. Life is constantly changing, I tell them, but we don't want it to, which is why we habituate our behavior. What's the right thing to do one day may not be the right thing to do the next. I tell them that, right now, they're doing a good job working very hard at doing homework, working internships, caring for loved ones, participating in college athletics, all the things you do when you're in college. But you can't keep that pace going your entire life. At some point you need to learn to dial it back, and if you don't, you'll experience a breakdown, which is the body's way of forcing you to slow down. I'll tell them that I understand the need to work hard, but that you can't work hard all the time, forever.

Right now, I'm trying to bike to parks as often as possible, trying to establish a new pattern, one of sitting still, in the hope that this new habituated behavior will shine light on all my other behaviors. Taking the time to do this means spending less time on the other things I usually do. Choices are made. Change happens.

Last night I asked Sue if she thinks I'm becoming more serene. She had to think about it for a minute, and then she carefully told me that she sees that I'm emotionally more even tempered, but I'm also more distant. I asked for this information, and now I need to reflect on it as a way to change. It's not my intent to distance myself from Sue, though I can see how that would be a natural result of trying to become more aware of the bigger picture, less caught up in the daily grind that infiltrates our domestic life.

If I find heightened peace of mind, what does that mean for those I spend time with? Am I a better resource for them if I'm more serene, or does that serenity create an unwanted distance? Right now, the answers aren't obvious. I'm going to have to give it more thought, knowing that such thought is the reason Sue feels I'm distancing.

23.

I'm back at Vermond Park, though not at my favorite picnic table. A groundskeeper is weed-eating the buckthorn near the picnic table I like to frequent, which is great, because buckthorn is invasive, but the weed-eater is a loud distraction. Instead, I'm sitting at a bench just south of the table. It's also close to the edge of the cliff, a couple hundred feet of drop-off above the shore of Lake Michigan. Killdeer and dragonflies work the wind on the edge of the cliff, catching updrafts, seemingly just for pleasure, exercising their gift of flight.

My bench is not tranquil. Not far off, a grandmother is teaching her two granddaughters how to fly a kite. The process involves shouting and crying. The granddaughters, Zoe and Hailey, take turns, and it's not fair, according to Hailey, that Zoe's kite-flying attempts are going higher and lasting longer. The grandmother is doing her best to placate the children, but her communicative solution is one of matching their collective volume. I can't tell if they're enjoying themselves or not. Eventually, Hailey runs too close to the cliff, which frightens the grandmother, as it should, because Hailey, who looks to be four or five, quickly figures out that her grandmother doesn't want her near the cliff. The closer she approaches the edge, the more attention she gets, so much so that the grandmother has had enough and tells them both to get back in the minivan. They drive away, leaving me to listen instead to the waves crashing against the shoreline below.

If I were bikepacking with Evan right now in the Rockies, I wouldn't be in proximity to such drama. Instead, I'd just be biking with Evan, camping wherever we wanted, popping into small mountain towns in search of food and beer. That's the kind of experience I long for, the kind of experience I wanted to give to Evan. Yet here I am, in a public park, sharing this domestic space with whoever enters it.

It's good to write this down. It helps me understand the lack of empathy I have for the grandmother and the girls. I found their drama irritating. I'm trying to sit still, motionless, quiet. I don't want that type of drama. I'm drawn to this expansive view of Lake Michigan, the lake's horizon, the lake's varying shades of blue. But if I want to experience the Divine, I need to accept that the Divine is just as present in Hailey and Zoe as it is in Lake Michigan. From where I'm sitting, it's all one living organism, and you can't pick and choose which kinds of life you want to connect with.

I talk a lot with my ethics students about empathy, how it's the opposite of narcissism. If narcissism is a cause of evil in this world, then empathy would be the antidote to it. I explain the difference between empathy and sympathy: that empathy generally requires a shared experience in order to find the connection. I can empathize with the grandmother, because Kait and Evan were once the ages Hailey and Zoe are now. I found myself remembering similar experiences when I was raising my children, the countless times we'd bicycle to a local park for a picnic or swim. They are good memories: It's good to remember how hard it was to get everyone to the park, to prepare the picnic, to keep a vigilant eye on the kids. I'm grateful that Kait and Evan are grown and on their own. It's good to have them still in my life, though I must admit that it's much, much easier to be their parent now that they are functional adults living in other parts of the country.

Sympathy: I can only sympathize with the killdeer and dragonflies that hover above the cliff, because I can't share in their activity of flying, which is why I sit here admiring them so. I recognize what it must be like to fly, but I do not know the emotion of flight.

Empathy: I empathize with the grandmother telling her grandkids to get back in the car because playtime is over. I also empathize with her pleasure in playing with her granddaughters, watching the girls marvel at her skill in getting the kite to fly high above the ground.

Over the years, I've taken engineering students on overseas service trips. I took mechanical engineering students to Kenya to build a school, took computer engineering students to northern India so they could build a computer lab for Buddhist nuns so they could communicate with Tibetan refugees trying to escape China, worked with all kinds of students in Guatemala doing medical projects for a nonprofit called Global Brigades. It was always difficult to go on those trips, difficult to exercise empathy with the people we worked with in these developing countries. I wanted to enable the students to leverage their academic training for the benefit of the communities they served, but the real intent of the service trips was to help the students empathize, or at least sympathize, with people in other countries.

I felt it was important to engage in the international trips because students taking part couldn't escape the experience. If you engage in community service in the city you live in, you engage in service for an afternoon at the most. When the service is over, you go home to the life you're comfortable with. International service isn't like that; you're always immersed. That's why I believe it's transformative. And, as an educator, I'm interested in cultural, empathetic transformation.

That's why I wanted to take Evan on the Great Divide ride: so he could meet other bikepackers, so he could be enveloped in the Rocky Mountains for several months at an impressionable time in his life. I wanted that experience for myself as well.

I can't be upset that I'm limited to these park experiences. It's not as extreme as the Rockies or Kenya or India, but there is knowledge here that I can learn from. It could be that it's easier to empathize in extremely different settings; it could be that it's more difficult to find that connection in the domestic, the local. But it shouldn't matter where I am. And to understand what that means I need to keep sitting here, looking over Lake Michigan, and be present despite the presence of screaming kite-flying children, knowing they are part of the world I'm learning to connect with.

24.

Today's Monday. I enjoyed another morning conversation with my friend Mark, followed by a trip to the office at the downtown university campus, where I reread passages in Theodore Rothke's *The Far Field*. I had a hard time connecting to the poems. I'm familiar with them, appreciate how their rhythm matches the imbalance in the poem's prose. But I didn't have much energy for reading poetry. Instead, I lay down on the floor and stared at the ceiling, something I tend to do when melancholic.

I tried escaping the melancholy by leaving the office, biking to a food truck and buying a burrito, then biking to Hubbard Park for a liter of Central Waters Rift IPA. The cure for a blue mood: burrito and a beer. But at the beer garden was a mother with three children. She was texting on her phone while her kids played hide and seek, running amid the garden's picnic tables, hiding in proximity to everyone here who's just trying to enjoy the park and the beer. It reminds me of the other day at Vermond Park, the grandmother flying a kite with her grandchildren. Kids making noise. Parents and grandparents, yelling at them to quiet down.

It makes me wonder if I was a nonstop noise machine when I was a kid. I'm surprised this boisterous scene is not upsetting me; maybe it's the melancholic mood overwhelming the beer garden's volume. I know that soon the mother will take her screaming children back to their car and drive home.

Seven point eight billion people live on this planet, a number that's doubled in my lifetime. There are so many of us. I enjoy biking into Milwaukee, visiting with Mark, spending time in a quiet office, in this beer garden. I'm glad Sue and I moved to Mequon, our acre of solitude. One's setting has such an impact on one's emotions.

I'm glad my reaction is one of melancholy rather than frustration or anger. Anger seems to be the antithesis of serenity. Melancholy seems to swim in the same waters as serenity. It's not as easy to tell if I'm melancholic when I'm alone, maybe because this emotion is such a part of me. It becomes apparent in the company of others.

Those kids may be loud, but they're having a good time. Hide and seek: what a great game. I wonder if I was melancholic as a child. I remember spending a lot of time playing alone, the youngest of four. I remember riding my bike more than playing with childhood friends. Biking alone to local parks – not much different from what I'm doing now.

If I was a melancholic child, I surely wasn't aware of it. I didn't learn the word "melancholy" until college, and as soon as I learned it, I knew what it was and that it was me. I learned the word when I switched majors to English, when I started to empathize with literary protagonists that were melancholic—the main characters in *The Awakening, Anna Karenina, Heart of Darkness*. These books helped me understand myself in ways that my psychologists couldn't. No one tells you they are steeped in melancholy, but you sure see it when you identify with the protagonists in these works of literature.

Spending time in silence, this exercise in just sitting, is good for the melancholy. It doesn't make it go away, but it provides the space for it to reside.

25.

I biked to Port Washington this morning and am sitting in an Adirondack chair, in the shade, in an empty beer garden just outside Inventors Brew Pub. The brewery doesn't open for another five hours, which gives me plenty of time simply to sit. I left the house with Sue and biked with her to her work. As we biked I said, "It's nice, the two of us cycling to work together." She looked at me and rolled her eyes.

I know Sue doesn't think that what I'm doing right now is "work," bicycling to parks so I can sit still for a couple of hours and then write some thoughts. But it is work and, right now, it's the best kind of work I can think of. To write about serenity, one must first be serene, and I can think of no better way to exercise daily peace of mind than biking, sitting, reflecting, and writing. All my favorite things in one daylong activity.

I can't blame her for the eye roll. Her business is exploding. She has more clients than she knows what to do with, has booked client appointments weeks in advance. I keep telling her that it's a nice problem to have. She keeps telling me that it's a problem nonetheless.

In a month I'll be busy again with teaching, committee work, office hours, faculty development initiatives. I'll be as hurried as she is. I can think of no better way to prepare for the busy season than doing what I'm doing now. Three months of biking and sitting should get me through the nine months of an academic schedule. It would be interesting to track how long I can go until I feel intellectually overwhelmed, sleep deprived, stressed. My hope is that I change the schedule, to incorporate ongoing biking and sitting exercises. I'd have to let go of some of my commitments, make time for this new habituated behavior.

I like what this is doing to me. Sue pointed out that it's making me a bit distant, but I think that's not altogether a bad thing. We've been married for over thirty years. Even though we both continue to evolve individually, we seem to do so without risking the relationship. If I were becoming more distant as the result of being more self-focused, then there would be cause for concern. Instead, I think I'm just being more present, which means being less conversational. I'm listening as much as I ever have, just not saying as much.

I've never been one for small talk. If there's a downside to this "serenity thought experiment," it may be that talk, conversation in general, is getting smaller and smaller.

I'm enjoying my time with Sue more than ever, especially when we don't have a need to say anything to each other.

There's a rhetorical pattern that I call the "I, me, my syndrome." Sometimes, I notice that the person I'm talking to is over-using the first-person pronoun. Sometimes people use it every third word or so, usually when they're describing themselves or telling a story in which they're the main character. I've often wondered if it's a cultural issue, American individualism and narcissism.

You can't escape the first-person pronoun. I've often tried speaking without it, only to realize how difficult that is to do. It's easier not to speak. Abe Masao, one of Nishida Kitaro's colleagues, wrote about this in *Zen and Western Thought*:

> The "I" is the basis of discrimination, placing itself as the center of everything. ... To be human is to be a problem to oneself, regardless of one's culture, class, sex, nationality, or the era in which one lives. To be human means to be an ego-self; to be an ego-self means

to be cut off from both one's self and one's world; and to be cut off from one's self and one's world means to be in constant anxiety. This is the human predicament.

The more time I spend sitting in parks, the more I realize that sitting alone in parks minimizes the I, me, my. In the park I'm not the protagonist; I'm simply one of many things, a human body among trees, bushes, lawn, birds, and insects, just one of many things. And the more I feel connected to the park, the less I am anxious, which enables prolonged depth in this activity of simply sitting.

Masao goes on to write about how egolessness is paradoxical: "For the individual to be truly an individual, it must be identical—paradoxically—with the absolute, while at the same time retaining its integrity as an individual. On the other hand, for the absolute to be really absolute, it must be identical—again, paradoxically—with the individual, while retaining its absolute character." I am the park, the park am I, and the more I sit here, the more I forget "I" am here, the more it's just the park. Yet "I" am still sitting in the park. The paradox presents itself when I define myself separate from the park.

Which takes me back to my life with Sue. She helps me be me, which involves finding myself beyond myself, in the "absolute," I practice in this park and bring the practice back home and share it with Sue.

26.

I'm back in Oostburg, at the picnic table beneath the evergreens, between the church parking lot and a baseball field. I wanted to bike through the soy and cornfields, past the cows and horses, the grain silos that surround this small farming town. It's about a twenty-five-mile ride to get here on the route I chose, about an hour and a half of cycling, enough time to get my head prepared for sitting still at this table.

The table is one of my favorites: green with algae, weathered boards, deck screws barely holding it together.

The cicadas are deafening. Their song usually makes for a pleasant background sound, but the volume today brings it to the forefront. Farming trucks roll down the one road running through town, and I can't hear them, just cicadas.

I've been thinking about what I wrote yesterday, about egolessness and extinguishing the "I". It's a difficult idea to get your head wrapped around. Not only is our culture rooted in individualism, but our philosophers are too. It goes back to the Greeks—Plato, Aristotle, Phaedrus—and continues through contemporary philosophers, theologians, and psychologists: Kant, Hume, Kierkegaard, *Nietzsche*, Freud. The eastern philosophers I read in graduate school explained a different way of viewing the world, one in which "ego" is nothing more than a phonetic symbol, an idea, not something that is real.

I talk to my ethics students about what is real and what is ethereal, how sometimes we create ideas as a way of explaining reality. Before Copernicus, the world was flat, and after Copernicus, it was round. Before Einstein, we believed in Newton's formula for gravity, a formula that works to a point, until you take into account that space and time are curved. Scientists keep coming up with better explanations as to what the world is. Science, like everything else, is in a constant state of change.

For the first couple of decades of my life I believed that I had a soul separate from everyone else's soul. That changed when I read Nishida, Suzuki, Nishitani, Tanabe, Dogen – all these Buddhists providing an alternate perspective on how things are, a perspective that helped me connect to just about everything. I don't want to have a soul separate from the souls of others. I don't want to worry about whose soul is saved or not. It was pretty easy to let all of that go.

It's still difficult to not view myself as separate from everyone else, probably because everyone I know believes they have a distinct and unique definition of soul and self.

There are downsides to having an ego separate from everyone else's ego. Competition, strife, the inability to understand each other: it's all rooted in separate egos. I tell my students that all of the "isms" – sexism, racism, ageism – are rooted in you viewing yourself separate from who I am, and you viewing your needs as more important than mine. This is more obvious now than ever. The pandemic, and the death of George Floyd, seem to make the isms more obvious, or unobvious, depending on how you choose to explain what's going on.

If I want my ethics students to do good, to conduct themselves in such a way that what they do makes the world a better place, then I tell them to look at what connects us.

It's not rational to view the world without a clear and distinct individual sense of egoistic self, and our western culture is rooted in the rational. If a western rational approach worked, if we could rationalize right from wrong, good from evil, then our world would be in better shape, and I probably wouldn't have to teach ethics classes.

Rationality tends to separate one from another. Or, as Nishida would say, it separates the subject from the object. The answer to finding "the good" must be rooted not in the rational, but in the intuitive. Not the mystical, since western society tends to confuse intuition with mysticism. Rather, it's simply more of a non-binary, non-linguistic connection with all things, be it my neighbor, my cat, my wife – whatever helps me extinguish the separation between you and "me, I, my."

27.

I'm not sitting at a picnic table in a park. Instead I'm at my favorite bar, Café Hollander, having a whit, a top-fermented wheat beer, brewed in Ertvelde, Belgium. When I left the house, I set a route on the cycling computer for a forty-mile ride, heading west through Germantown and Jackson, but a mile into the ride, I realized that today isn't the day for big bike miles. I wanted to get back to thinking, or intuiting, about intuition and why I view it as a pathway to exercising good conduct, and this feels like the right place to do it. I like this bar because it has garage doors for walls, doors that are currently wide open, allowing a nice breeze to blow from one end of the bar to the other, a happy blend of indoor and outdoor, a safe place to enjoy good beer in a pandemic.

The disadvantage of sitting in a bar is the near impossibility of simply sitting. The sitting part is easy enough. The beer is good, and a couple of flat-screen televisions are airing tennis and World Cup soccer. No, the difficulty is thinking the way I want to when simply sitting. The whole point of sitting still is to get into a certain mental mindset, one that isn't rational but intuitive, one that's nice and slow and quiet. Though I love this bar, it's filled with mental stimulation, and the beauty of sitting in a park, where hopefully no one else is around, is the lack of mental stimulation, which makes it easier to engage in the intuitive and the divine.

It's difficult to explain intuition. I tell my students that we do teach them how to read and write, how to speak in public, but we don't teach them how to think, and as a result, we don't discuss the different ways of thinking. Universities are grounded in rational thought. Rational thought allows for correct answers. When I teach I'm rational, but I also teach my students the value of intuitive thought, because it's a different kind of thought experience, one that helps when rationality doesn't work, when the questions are larger or far from obvious.

When it comes to "doing good," when I'm conflicted as to how to conduct myself, or when I must decide on the right course of action, I rely on intuition more than on rational thought. Francis P. Cholle, author of *The Intuitive Compass*, writes about how we, as a culture, rely heavily on rational thought and often suppress our intuitive, inner voice. He defines intuition as "a process that gives us the ability to know something directly without analytic reasoning, bridging the gap between the conscious and nonconscious parts of our mind, and also between instinct and reason." To make good decisions and act accordingly, we need both instinct and reason.

It isn't an either/or thing, either rational or intuitive. The brain can do both at the same time. My argument with my students (and it is an argument, because they believe deeply in limiting one's thoughts to the rational, as if intuitive thought puts rational thought at risk somehow) is that we can't help being rational. It's the human predicament, the result of an overly developed cortex. But thinking rationally doesn't mean we should squelch intuition, especially when it comes to making good decisions and acting on good decisions.

It takes time to develop one's intuition. Just sitting is an important tool to developing it, to just sit and be present, mentally awake but not thinking about anything in particular. To minimize the stimulus.

I gave a lecture on this topic last year in an Eastern Philosophy class, how the East isn't as rooted in the rational, how intuition is more of a philosophical tool, and how they can use that tool whenever they want—though, like any tool, you need to use it in order to know how to use it. The students asked if I would give them class time to simply sit and intuit. It was easy for me to say "yes", because I could spend the time modeling intuitive thought for them, since "just sitting" is my jam.

It was a ninety-minute class. We spent sixty minutes sitting still, then thirty minutes talking in small groups and then in a large group. They found it difficult at first, but once they sat still long enough, it simply began to happen. They told each other, and then me, that they wished they could do this more often—if only they had the time. I told them that they just need to make time to do it. They pushed back on that assertion, telling me that their hectic schedules cannot accommodate it. I suggested dialing back on their social media as a way of finding time to engage in intuitive thought, but that idea didn't stick. I told them that it doesn't have to be a full sixty minutes. It could be just ten minutes a day.

I lectured, or preached to a degree, that to develop one's intuitive skills, you need to be intentional about it. Yes, spend time "just sitting" and try to quiet the mind, but also be aware of what it does to your thought process. When making decisions, be aware of how you are making them. Are you relying on reason alone, or are there other tools you can use?

As the semester continued, we would periodically take ten minutes to simply sit still, usually when the students asked that we do so because they were mentally tired and needed a refresh to best discuss the day's material. I wasn't sure if I was teaching them anything per se, maybe just giving them the opportunity to do what we had talked about, to engage in conduct based on the idea of good behavior: in this instance good behavior taking the form of sitting still and trying not to think about anything in particular.

I'd tell them that, yes, they were meditating. But I also told them that I don't like the way our Western culture has usurped the term "meditation" and the way people use it. We don't need pillows to sit on, no need to sit in a full lotus position. Those tools and techniques have helped people meditate for centuries, but they are not prerequisites to simply sit still. It's so easy, I tell them, but so hard, the difficulty residing in our lack of experience, lack of practice, inability to not consume data, to put the smartphone down, to minimize the to-do list, to enjoy our own company once in a while.

28.

I'm back at the Hubbard Park Beer Garden, but this time I came when the garden's closed, so the entire garden is mine. Out of respect for this being a beer garden, I brought a can of beer, an Oskar Blues Can-O-Bliss Hazy India Pale Ale. I love good beer. It doesn't matter that it's warm, the can having sat in my bike-bag for the last couple of hours as I've been cycling about and having yet another Monday morning conversation with Mark Zimmerman.

Mark and I talked once more about the pandemic and politics, how people are turning face masks into political theatre, how the president is sending federal soldiers into cities whether there's protesting taking place or not, how it's nearly the end of July and a wave of people will soon be evicted from their homes. There's a lot to process right now, and Mark's a good person to process it with. He's someone who knows how to sit still. He reads and writes every day, activities that are reflective by nature. But what he chooses to read is prose and poetry written by authors who reflect, who strive to create material with substance and subtext. It's different from reading online, since most of that material is written in such a way that it doesn't require interpretation, or ask the reader to entwine with it.

I need to learn how to read and write for longer periods of time. I used to be able to read and write all day, back before the internet, before I owned a television, before the doctorate and the career in high tech. I can't blame technology for my inability to sit and read and write for hours at a time; it's my choice to engage the laptop, smart-phone, and fifty-five-inch flat-screen TV. It's my hope that this "sit-ting still" activity will engender an ability to read and write more and longer. I need to be aware of how these activities influence each other.

This morning, I'm rereading William Duggan's book on *Strategic Intuition* for several hours. It's a book I've read countless times, a required text when teaching a course in Creative Thinking. Rereading is easier than reading, because you reintroduce yourself to ideas you're already familiar with. It's like my weekly conversations with Mark: We talk about the same basic stuff. It's not new, and I like that. It would be different if I were meeting someone I didn't know for the first time, someone I wanted to get to know. That requires more mental effort, more short-term memory rather than long-term memory. And right now I'd rather put mental effort into sitting still, into writing and reading about what happens when you simply sit still, which is why I reread Duggan.

He introduces several terms that help one understand how to intuit. The first term is "strategic intuition," a type of slow thinking that I've been practicing all summer. He writes that it's different from ordinary intuition: "Ordinary intuition is a form of emotion: feeling, not thinking. Strategic intuition is the opposite: it's think-ing, not feeling." He differentiates strategic intuition from "expert intuition," which is a "form of rapid thinking where you jump to a conclusion when you recognize something familiar." In short, stra-tegic thinking is slow and works well to solve big problems, where you want your brain to take all of the ideas and thoughts residing in it and connect them in such a way that epiphanies become possible. Expert intuition, in comparison, works well for solving small prob-lems, because it focuses on quick, rational thought. Most of what my students learn is rooted in expert intuition. They memorize facts for quizzes and tests, write lab reports that are a mere page in length, deliver ten-minute presentations. Lots of brief activities. And it's good training for their future careers; they'll probably spend their entire lives solving lots of small problems. I tell them that I'm not dissing this way of thinking; I just don't find it nearly as interesting as solving large problems, in exercising slow, intuitive thought.

I'm trying to become serene, which is no small task. The more I strive for peace of mind, the more I realize it can be an all-consuming activity. The more you do it, the more you want to do it.

Acknowledging that I was not serene six months ago, when the pandemic became real, and wanting to figure out a formula for serenity, was a way of defining a "problem of scale." Researching "serenity" became the first step in the process, putting data into my short-term memory and letting it stew for a while. Exercising strategic intuition and "just sitting" became the next step: sit still and let the data connect. But to let all that information connect, and to let new ideas germinate, you have to give your brain some space. You must minimize the stimulation. And, as I've learned this summer, you must give it the kind of open space the brain needs to work at its best.

That's why these picnic tables serve as tools for a specific type of thought process. I'm outdoors, so I can hear the wind in the trees and the birds chirping. I can watch the slow-moving Milwaukee River. I can feel the influence of this setting, its slow and steady pace.

29.

I'm at the Fusion Soccer Club, a half-dozen abandoned soccer fields with a covered picnic area in the center. More than a hundred barn swallows dart about. Their mud nests line the eaves of this covered picnic area, probably because this facility hasn't been used this year. I've been here for a while, watching a westerly wind blow cloud cover toward Lake Michigan, watching a variety of deciduous trees that frame the park bend in the wind, watching the barn swallows. I'll watch one barn swallow move its way above the grass fields, darting among the other barn swallows, and then watch all of the barn swallows at once, following their swirling patterns.

This sitting activity has become addictive. I must remind myself to write down the ideas that pass through my mind. Not that I have to write them down, but I do enjoy seeing them in sentences. When I started this project, I thought that simply sitting would be a great vehicle for the writing process. Now I'm wondering if the reverse is true, if writing what I think about when sitting still encourages me to sit still more, as well as documenting the thought process. The two activities seem mutually beneficial.

There's also a lack of drama in these activities, which is good in a time of pandemic, cultural unrest, and political theatre. If I want to understand the drama of these times, it seems that engaging in low stimulus activities helps one find answers. It's good to gather the data, to watch the evening news to find out where the pandemic is spreading or where the social protests are raging. But always consuming data doesn't help you make sense of it. It's like drinking beer: you can't just drink, and drink, and drink, and appreciate the beer. Best to drink a beer that demands appreciation, then stop and make sense of its nuance. Today's beer, for example, is a One-Y Hazy India Pale Ale: not too heavy, yet a hefty hop-feel at the end. I'm drinking out of a can, which makes it impossible to appreciate its hazy, New England color. It's also difficult to gather its aroma through the can's opening. If I were a better beer consumer, I'd bring a glass with me for the sake of visual and olfactory appreciation. But there's enough to appreciate here. By minimizing the drama to wind, barn swallows, and hazy IPA, I focus in on them.

It takes time to watch a bank of clouds cross the sky, but I've given myself enough time to view it. It reminds me of solo bike touring: you roll into a campsite, set up your tent, make some food, crack open a beer, and take in what the campsite has to offer. Maybe that's a reason I'm attracted to sitting at these picnic tables: its local simulation of cross-country bike travel. I know that I enjoy bike touring and bikepacking because of the thought process that goes into these activities, learning how to sit in a saddle for nine-hour stretches, being alone with one's thoughts. I'm happy to find some of that experience in these domestic sitting activities: you can't always go off on a bike tour. It takes planning, timing, resources. And you must be away from the ones you love for weeks or months at a time. A big perk of what I'm currently doing is going home and seeing Sue every night. I could always bike tour with her, but then we'd always be together. And, as I've mentioned before, I enjoy the balance between being alone and being with her.

A couple of years ago I started a consulting practice, Epiphany Consulting. In my Creative Thinking classes I had had success helping students engage in strategic intuition, having them define problems of scale and gather data that could help them solve large problems, then giving them time to not think about the problems, time to let their brains make sense of the problem's data. I would have them leave their phones and computers in the classroom and go for a walk outside, or head over to the university's art museum and sit in front of a painting, or find a bench in downtown Milwaukee and ask them to close their eyes and think as little as possible. The students loved these activities, in part because they were wildly different from the experiences they had in their other university courses, but also because they would have ideas regarding the problems they were trying to solve. Most of the time their ideas were not directly related to the problem, so I would have them write about the problem, and about their ideas, as a way of helping them see that the problem they were trying to solve usually wasn't the problem they wanted to solve, because it wasn't what their brains thought about when given the opportunity to just sit still and let the brain do what it does.

The consulting practice lasted only a year but was a good experience. After working with a half-dozen clients, I realized that adults aren't as disciplined as students are when it comes to learning. If I told a student to take an hour and go for a walk, they'd usually do it, but my clients wouldn't follow the same advice. I'm sure it had a lot to do with the dynamics of the classroom, the professor/student relationship, how students don't usually question their faculty when they're told what to do, especially when grading is involved. My clients, in contrast, struggled to find the time or inclination to simply sit on a bench or go for a long walk alone. But most important, the clients struggled to adapt to the thought process, the ability to slow one's thoughts down.

I'm sure it has to do with being older. Young people's brains are more malleable. They have more neuroplasticity, and they don't have decades of habituated thought processes. It's more difficult for someone my age to learn to think differently, just as it's more difficult to learn a new language or how to play a new musical instrument. It's possible, but you must create new neurological pathways in your brain. Doing that requires a heightened degree of intentionality and discipline.

There were some successes. One client was faced with the problem of trying to decide whether to sell his business. He was at retirement age and was growing tired of the daily grind. But the company that wanted to buy his practice told him they were most interested in his client base, that they would morph the company into something more profitable and would follow a different business model and mission statement. We had weekly phone calls to talk about what he was writing down in his thought journal, tracking every thought he had about the problem and its potential solution. I told him it would take some time to find the answer. The bigger the problem, the more time it usually takes. And for him this was a big one, since he defined himself in his business.

We took a few weeks off from our weekly calls when I went on a six-week bike tour with Kait. Toward the end of the tour, I called him from a café in Missoula. He told me he had found the solution to the problem: don't sell the business, at least not yet. Enjoy it for a few more years and see if other buyers would present themselves. He said that the answer didn't come all at once in an epiphany, which disappointed him a bit. I told him that sometimes the answers come all at once, but at other times they come in a series of smaller revelations. Regardless, he was happy to have solved the problem.

He ended up selling the business a year later to the same people that had made him the initial offer. By waiting a bit, he was able to negotiate for a better offer as well as for the ability to continue working in the company for a few more years, so he could save a bit more for retirement and have a designated exit strategy for a career that spanned the entirety of his adult life.

Other clients were less successful. One was tired of the demands of her job that required her to drive six days a week, meeting with customers in three states. While she drove she was on the phone, talking to other potential customers or using her phone for audio dictation. She was exhausted. But she was making good money, and she needed to find a new career that provided the same income. It also would take time, not only to gather the data needed to find the new job but to slow her brain down, to sit still, to ruminate about it. She never found the time; her job didn't allow for it. She never solved the problem. She's still working the same job.

I learned from the consulting experience. For what I want from a career, teaching trumps consulting. Regardless of what it is I'm teaching, I always end up talking about how the brain works and how we can slow our thought process down as a way of problem solving. All my classes have to do with high order thought process, helping students become what the university calls "self-directed learners."

College students are more open to trying new ways of thinking. They're also generally tired of always engaging in Duggan's "expert intuition," of memorizing information for the sake of solving small academic problems. I tell them expert intuition isn't a bad thing, but it's only one tool in your cognitive toolbox, and it's not a very good tool to use when solving problems of scale. Strategic intuition is better suited for that. And, I tell them, it's more interesting to have a career where you get to solve problems of scale. Not just because it's fun to have epiphanies, to be the "idea guy," but because you tend to have more impact.

I tell them there's a reason people who do well in business have the corner office. It's because corner offices have great windows, and smart people know how to use windows as a tool for thinking. Just gazing out the window is a great way to solve big problems. Not everyone has the knack for it. When I worked at Microsoft, I knew some of the intellectual drivers in my group, and they were often solitary people, introverts who loved to read and think. It wasn't an oddity to walk past an office and see one of them facing the window, away from their computer monitors and whiteboards. I was envious, because my job at the time involved a ton of expert intuition.

I was lucky, though. My group experienced an internal takeover. Leadership from another part of the company fired our leaders because the new leaders wanted credit for the project. It took the new leadership six months to understand the technology we were creating, and during that time, I had nothing to do. My manager told me to just look busy, a skill I'm not good at, so I thought a lot during those six months about my job and how I wanted to do work that required slower thought, to solve different problems. It led to an epiphany: find a new career that requires you to think slowly.

30.

I'm at Brown Deer Park, the largest park I've been to this summer. It has a golf course, frisbee golf course, lake, baseball fields, soccer fields, and countless picnic tables. I biked around the park for a half-hour before deciding to sit near the lake, near a grove of trees, only to discover within a few minutes that the mosquitos were making the most of the lake before they made the most of me. I moved to another part of the park, equally empty, this spot in the shade yet on the edge of a field filled with sunshine and fresh-mown grass. Maple trees are everywhere. It's only five miles from my home, yet I've never explored this park.

It reminds me of Lincoln Park, the park I'd go to when I was a kid living in West Seattle. Like this park, Lincoln Park was expansive, even more so given that I was all of ten or twelve years old. I'd go to the pool, swim with my friends or by myself, then find a place in the park to sit. Funny how sitting in parks this summer brings back the emotions and memories of childhood. I'm not sure I ever realized how much time I spent alone.

When I was a kid, I could just hop on my bike and go anywhere I wanted, as long as I was home before dinner. Maybe now I'm following the same set of rules. Maybe that's why this feels like summer.

I think I found my career, professing, in part because it lends itself to solitude. I figure out lesson plans by myself, read texts by myself, sit in my office during office hours waiting for students to drop in—by myself. Maybe solitude is a bit of a career hazard. I have plenty of colleagues who are social creatures, who want to meet and talk about pedagogy and shared readings. I can do that to a point, but I typically excuse myself and return to the office, close the office door, and look out the window.

Now that there's a pandemic, I'm not returning to campus, possibly for another year, teaching online from anywhere that has internet. It would be interesting to use my phone as a hotspot to go online from a park such as this, but I don't think it would work. I've tried teaching classes outdoors in the past, have brought groups of students to the parks near campus. Everyone just gets distracted, realizes just how much they'd rather be doing outdoor things.

I'm tired, a good type of tired. The air's humid, the sun hot, the cicadas deafening. On the way here, I went by a local deli and bought a pastrami sandwich and a Bell's Hopsolution Ale, a double IPA. The nice thing about giving yourself time to sit in the middle of a park is that you can slowly enjoy a good sandwich and beer.

I'm tired because I spent the morning fixing the tubeless front tire on my adventure bike. Four days ago, I took it apart to see how a tubeless setup worked, and in the process couldn't put it back together again. Over the last couple of days, I've watched YouTube videos on how to go through the procedure, but the expertise of the videographers just frustrated me, their familiarity with the process, how easy they made it look. I'd go back to the garage and try to put the tire back together again, only to fail, the bead between the tire and rim not holding air. After failing again this morning, I went back in the house and lay down on the couch, trying to empty my head of the frustration. After a bit, I decided to try reading instructions instead of watching videos. I found a website that explained the six-step procedure: clean the rim and rim-tape with rubbing alcohol, put the tape in the rim, put the valve in, put the tire on, add the sealant through the valve, pump up the tire with an air compressor. The beauty of reading, as opposed to watching videos, is that I can do it at my own slow pace. I thought about each step in the process, thought about how I'd done it wrong previously, and imagined the correct method. Still, on returning to the garage I had to go through the steps several more times. I stayed calm, and when I would feel frustration coming on I walked away.

I'm not mechanically inclined, and I know that the best way to become mechanical is to do the mechanics. I tell students that making mistakes is a good thing and is part of the learning process. What I don't tell them is that learning is hard, and you can't avoid it, not if you want to master the application. M. Scott Peck said life is difficult until you accept the fact that life is difficult. In this instance, learning how to fix a tubeless bike tire was difficult until I finally accepted the fact that it's difficult. Once I accepted that, I went back to the garage, and within ten minutes the tire was inflated and good to go.

I'd rather learn how to fix a flat tire on a tubeless setup in my garage than bring it to the bike shop and ask them to fix it for me, and I'd rather learn how to fix it in the garage than on a gravel road in the middle of nowhere. Riding tubeless has great advantages: it gives the bike more "bike feel," it's much less likely to get a flat, it lessens the weight of the rim, and you can run lower pounds per square inch, which equates to better suspension. I love learning about bikes, and I love when I can figure it out by myself, even though it can be frustrating.

It's not uncommon that I give up, take the bike to the bike shop, and ask them to fix it. Sometimes, that's the best way to find out how to fix the bike, to watch someone who knows what they're doing do it, so I can give it another go the next time the issue presents itself.

I've been wrenching on bikes most of my life, and I always seem to need to learn something new. It's one of the reasons I love cycling. The few things I love deeply require an ongoing learning curve. Does "peace of mind" follow once the problem is solved? Yes, especially if the process of fixing the tire is slow, if I have the time to make mistakes, reflect, learn from them, and try again. Will it be more likely that I have "peace of mind" the next time I try to fix a tubeless tire? Yes, because I won't have to learn so much, which will enable me to enjoy the process of doing bike maintenance without having to strain my brain. Will I enjoy riding the bike more, knowing I fixed it? Yes. If the tire flats while I'm on a ride, I'll know how to fix it, and that means less cycling anxiety.

The reverse is true too. When I'm anxious while trying to fix the flat, when I try to hurry it along, when I get frustrated and angry with the process and my inability to solve the problem, I give up and take it to the shop to have them fix it, which takes away my confidence in my desire to learn more about bikes.

If I hadn't fixed the flat, I wouldn't have been able to ride the bike to this park. I could have ridden one of my other bikes, but there was satisfaction in riding this one today. It's important to recognize accomplishment, even for something as small as fixing a flat. The more it's recognized, the easier it is to delve into the next variable, easier to make more mistakes, easier to learn more about the bike.

31.

I biked up to Port Washington, a longer ride with a headwind, but my legs are feeling good, the net result of biking daily to these parks I'm becoming intimate with. I'm back at Inventors Brewery, this time arriving when they're open. There's music playing, country and pop, which isn't my preference, and there's a handful of people enjoying the beer and burgers. It's a good change of pace compared to the isolation and solitude I've been seeking this summer. I'm enjoying a nice amber ale. Inventors is a single batch brewery: their taps rotate frequently since they make small, quality production beer.

The "serenity experiment" is working. Yesterday, I was moving some brewing equipment from the basement to the garage to prepare for brewing some beer next weekend, and I dropped a corny keg on my foot while going down the stairs. I also dropped a few *Fucks!*, but I quickly realized that I'd done so. That immediate realization isn't typical, and it was rewarding to realize the realization: There was no need to be upset, no need for expletives, to react in frustration, because I didn't intend to drop the keg. I was just moving too quickly, wasn't aware of what I was doing, which meant I wasn't doing it well.

Realtime reactions say a lot about a person. It's not uncommon for me to react with profanity, especially when I'm alone.

I don't feel anxious, not the way I was when this pandemic began, when I was working to help many of my faculty colleagues jump to an all-online teaching format. It wasn't just the faculty: my students were also anxious about going online, about moving off campus and back to their homes, their families, homes that were typically crowded, sharing bandwidth both mentally and digitally. That seems like a long time ago. I know the university will start up again in a month, and even though the university's strategy is to adopt a hybrid model, blending on-site with online, my hunch is that the pandemic will surge again and we'll return to an all-online format.

It will be different this time around. In the spring, I gave up a job as the Associate Director for Faculty Development. It was an important job, one I believed in, helping faculty figure out how to meet the needs of our students through interactive classroom dynamics. But it was too demanding, and it was depleting me. I couldn't stop thinking about work, couldn't stay away from email, meetings, and documentation. I was far from serene and opted to go back to teaching and researching, roles I'm familiar with, tasks that are more mentally manageable. I won't make as much money, but I don't need to make more money. Sue and I moved to a less expensive home, in a county that has lower taxes, and opted to let go of one of our cars. It's a less expensive lifestyle. Besides, the governor's "stay at home" pandemic policy prevents me from going out and dropping cash on extravagances.

There's no guarantee that I'll keep this job, given the pandemic, the uncertainty, the volatility of the economy. But for now it's less work and, as they say, less is more.

I'm beginning to wonder what would happen if I lost my job, if the university had to cut back on faculty due to decreasing enrollment numbers. It's happening to universities and colleges across the country, especially those with small endowments. Would I lose my sense of self if I lost my job, a profession I deeply identify with and believe in, the preoccupation I've delved into for three decades?

I like to think that I'd survive it, that my work does not define me. I have to think like this, because I want to be aware of those variables that can take away the peace of mind I've engendered. Losing the job would be such a variable.

Losing Sue would be another such variable. If she left me for another man or woman, or if she just left me altogether, how would I respond? What would happen if we lost one of our children? It's an interesting thought experiment, to imagine what would happen. Not to be masochistic, but to know what defines me. And if I were to lose what defines me, my work and wife, my children, would it ruin me?

The problem with defining one's self in externals—work, family, possessions—is that there is no control over the external. Nishida wrote that we "cannot freely control all things in the external world. … The only things we can freely manage are our own phenomena of consciousness." I am what's inside me, not what's outside me. That's a difficult idea to get your head wrapped around when you live in a culture that places emphasis on the external. But I find it to be a healthy perspective. I don't want anxiety, and anxiety is driven by external variables. This pandemic is a perfect example. If you had told me six months ago that I wouldn't be going to my office for the next year, that I wouldn't be biking through the Rocky Mountains this summer, that I'd be wearing a mask wherever I go and staying a healthy distance away from anyone who's not in my inner circle, I wouldn't have believed you. So much has happened in such a small amount of time. It's been difficult to adapt to the change; it's created anxiety. But anxiety is internal, a response to external variables, and the more I understand the anxiety in relation to "self," the better I can see it for what it is and then minimize it.

Biking solo, sitting still, getting reflective, writing it all down, is giving an emphasis and appreciation for the inner self. It's correlation with these environments I find myself in, the parks and beer gardens, Lake Michigan and the Milwaukee River. This moment in the sun, at this picnic table, enjoying a small-batch amber beer.

32.

Today's a bit different. I biked to my office on campus. It's Monday. The museum my office is in is open Tuesday through Saturday; I go to the office on Mondays so I have the entire empty building to myself. It's wonderfully quiet, an empty art museum.

During the school year I'll sit alone in my office for hours at a time, working or not working. When I'm not working, I turn the computer off, turn the ringer on the phone off, dim the shades on the window, put my feet up on the desk, and just sit still. Sometimes it feels wrong, because there's plenty of work to do. But I need to do it. If I'm rested (that's really what I'm doing, resting), then I'm ready to work hard when it's time to work hard. But I must let the mind be as still as the body, as the stillness of the workspace.

Work culture is weird in twenty-first-century America. You're praised for working too much, for being hyper-productive. I enjoy the job security that comes with getting things done well, but I learned long ago, when I was finishing my dissertation, that you can't work hard all the time and expect to work well, especially when the work involves reading, writing, thinking, and listening.

Resting can be more difficult to enact than working. I get why it takes years of practice to learn to meditate. It's a way of thinking, and learning to manage one's thought process takes time and repetition. I think a lot about mental stimulation. It's been interesting, this summer, to sit for hours outside and try not to think about anything in order to be present in what I consider the Divine. Sitting in this office is different, because there is no natural stimulation. No barn swallows flying about here. No sunshine on my face or clouds slowly crossing the sky. It's just an indoor, unnatural sense of quiet. Unnatural because nature is never this quiet. Even when I wake in the middle of the night from some odd dream, go downstairs, and go out on the deck to look at the stars, there is much to consume. Not just the stars in their splendor, but the fireflies, sometimes hundreds of them, illuminating the backyard. The coyotes that often howl in the distance. The Canadian geese honking in the pond across the way. Last night, the crickets were deafening. It can be too much, too much of the Divine sometimes, and I have to return to the house.

How I think is not completely dependent on the stimulation I place myself in, but the setting has much to do with it. The importance of knowing how one thinks is that you can't control the stimulation around you. Nishida wrote that freedom comes not from without but from within. I long struggled with trying to find freedom. When I was young, I found freedom by moving away from home. Then I had to work and save money so I could travel, because travel, especially traveling alone, was "ultimate freedom." I could go where I wanted, when I wanted. What I didn't realize then, that I continue to try to realize now, is that I was just putting myself into a setting that allowed for a certain type of mental experience. It wasn't backpacking through Europe for five months that defined the freedom, so much as the way it made me think.

A few years ago I biked from Seattle, where I grew up, to Milwaukee, where I've lived for the last seventeen years. It was a solo bike ride, a thirty-two-day thought experiment. I wanted to know what I would think about if I were to sit in the saddle for nine hours a day. When I reflect on that wonderful month of my life, I realize that I was free. Not just because I could determine where I was going and how slowly I could get there, but because it made me think differently. It was that setting, all that open space, the Rocky Mountains and Great Plains, that made me think expansively. It was the setting. But you can't always backpack through Europe or bike across America. That's not normal life. Those are the rare opportunities you have to plan for and then enact with the hope that they will transform you. I want to think as I did on that big bike ride, and this summer of sitting in parks has brought me back to that thought process. And it's all the more freeing, because this summer I don't have the opportunity to bike across the country.

I can't control the pandemic or the economy. Businesses are shutting down. People are losing their jobs. If the students don't return to the university, then I'm out of a job too. That's beyond my control, and that sense of lost control takes away freedom, and feeling free is key to serenity.

Freedom isn't the space I'm in. Freedom comes from within. Nishida wrote that as "our knowledge advances, we become freer people. Even if we are controlled or oppressed by others, when we know this we extricate ourselves from the oppression. If we go even farther and realized the unavoidable reason for the situation, then the oppression turns into freedom."

I didn't come into the office today just to sit quietly in the office. There are things to do, a conference call about a scholarship we need to crowdfund for, a meeting with colleagues I'm sharing a virtual conference presentation with, syllabi to draft for fall courses, a new online learning management system to master. I have weeks of work to do. I don't want to be oppressed or overwhelmed by it, create anxiety about all that work. Rather, I want to be rested and ready to do this meaningful work. Work, regardless of what the work is, lacks meaning if you're not doing it willingly. The work can free me, but only if I approach it with the deep understanding that it is stimulation. And if I think about it a certain way, in an environment that lets me think well, then I can work well, and it won't stress or deplete me.

33.

I'm at River View Park, an odd name since buckthorn growing on the river's edge long ago eclipsed the view of the river. It's a quiet, small park not more than four miles from home. I'm disappointed not to have come here earlier this summer, because it's a park that always tends to be empty.

I've established a routine when it comes to simply sitting. When I leave the house I have an idea about where I'm going to go, but usually the destination changes once I'm on the bike. I'm not sure why this is, though I do like the idea that the location chooses me just as much as I choose the location. When I arrive I choose a picnic table (if there's more than one), lean my bike up against it, take out my laptop, reading glasses, and the beer I usually bring along, then sit down facing away from the computer, facing the expanse of the park.

I'll sit still for as long as possible. How long I sit depends solely on the mindset I'm bringing to the park. If my mind is already quiet, then I can sit still for over an hour. But if I'm anxious to write down an idea, well, I turn around, turn on the laptop, open this manuscript, and start to write.

Rereading these passages, I've noticed that the writing is better if I can sit still longer and delay the writing process. This shouldn't be any surprise. It's good to quiet the mind so that when it comes time to write, I can simply do it without thinking about what I'm doing. When writing isn't rational, when it's intuitive, the words take on a life of their own. I just have to prevent myself from getting in the way of the writing.

It's certainly a more enjoyable way to write, say, in comparison to writing based on an outline, where you organize all the ideas in advance in order to assure a rational, structured approach to the prose. That approach takes all the creativity and spontaneity out of the process, and writing should be creative when at all possible.

My freshmen who take Composition courses, which run the first semester of their first year, typically hate to write, in part because many of them haven't been asked to write beyond the five-paragraph essay format. You can't develop much of a thought when you can only write down a page of prose. I'll tell them that the five-para-graph essay is convenient for the teacher who has to grade too many essays. It doesn't make for good reading. And then I ask them if they believe their writing has ever been read for the sake of anything other than evaluation, and they typically say, in unison, "No."

It's an important conversation to have. Those freshmen know how to research, but research means turning to the ideas of others to defend one's idea. I try to get them to turn to their own ideas to defend their thesis, which is difficult to do if you're not familiar with your own thought process. It's why I tell them that learning to write is as much about learning how to think as it is learning how to master the English language. If you don't have something worth saying, then it's likely no one will read your work. And it helps, when writing, to believe you have a potential audience at the end of the process, some-one who will benefit from the documentation of your ideas.

It also helps to think in complete sentences. I ask all my students, regardless of what class I'm teaching, if they think in complete sentences. Few of them do. I tell them that it's easier to write in complete sentences if you think in them, and then we usually do some in-class thought exercises where they have to structure their thoughts around subjects and predicates, nouns and verbs. They'll tell me that it's difficult, and I'll tell them that I agree, changing the way you think is difficult, especially if you've never thought that way before. But over time it does impact the quality of their writing, because it makes writing easier. I tell them, "Easy is good." If it's easy for the writer to write, then it's likely going to be easier for the reader to read their writing.

If I truly believe in being serene, and if I believe that serenity leads to clearer thoughts, and as a result clearer writing, then I have to talk to the students about serenity. Waiting to write an essay the night before it's due isn't an approach that brings on serenity. When I was a student I would write that way, but that was a long time ago. What I'm doing now is the antithesis of that methodology. I'm giving myself an hour to bike to a location of my choice, an hour to sit and be present in that space, and then an hour or two to write. And if I can't write, then I read what I've written so far and revise.

It's an easy process to enact in the summer, when the schedule isn't as jampacked. But maybe the lesson to be learned here is to no longer enact a jampacked schedule. And by "jampacked," I mean thinking quickly all the time. I can have an event-filled day, and I can enact those events, but if I think in the right way, it's not exhausting. Some activities, such as teaching, do require quick thought, to respond to student questions, to listen to what they have to say, to negotiate text. It is mentally tiring, which is why I ensure that when I'm not teaching, I'm doing other activities that are not as mentally taxing, and in doing so strike that mental balance I'm looking for.

Much of it is physical. If you sleep well, then you awake rested. The body builds up glucose when you sleep. The brain can consume up to thirty percent of the body's glucose during the course of the day, so much of what I'm doing is glucose management. Think slowly, save the fuel the brain needs to perform at its peak, then use it when intended.

It takes great mental discipline, but it's doable. This pursuit of serenity that I'm enacting is nothing more than mental discipline: make the decision to think a certain way, think that way, and be self-aware enough to know when your thought process is off. And when it is off, self-correct, and go back to thinking clearly, slowly.

This thought experiment is teaching me that thought, like action, is habituated. The more I sit still in parks, the easier it is to think slowly when I'm not in parks. Take, for example, weeding. Sue and I bought our home last winter and had a lawn service remove as much buckthorn as possible in the spring. Buckthorn is a resilient, non-native species. It grows quickly, everywhere. Sue believes in managing the buckthorn in our one-acre yard, which come to find out is a nonstop activity. It's not as important to me, though I acknowledged how important it is to Sue.

Several weeks ago, I was talking about weeding buckthorn with Bob, who lives across the street. Bob's lived in the neighborhood for over forty years, having built his house and landscaped his yard. He told me: "It never ends. You're always keeping the buckthorn from growing over your property." I wasn't thrilled to hear this, though after thinking about it long enough, I realized that I just have to accept the fact that there is buckthorn, I am married to someone who wants to keep it from overrunning our property, and if I'm smart, I'll learn to go out and weed the yard without hesitation or angst.

I told Sue this morning that I'd weed today while she's at work. I know she'd love to come home to see a bucket full of weeds on the burn pile. Maybe I'll do a mini-thought experiment this afternoon: weed in such a way that it doesn't trouble me: serenely weed.

34.

I'm at Herman A. Zeunert Park in Cedarburg. I've been saving this park, a destination for a crisp, clear morning ride. It has a manmade lake at its center, with plenty of benches and picnic tables to view the lake and its surrounding fields of grass and trees. People are walking their dogs or going for a morning jog. I'm the only one sitting in the park, possibly because there's a chill in the air, the first morning this summer with temperatures in the low fifties. I love cold air, how it wakes you up, which is what I need this morning. Sue wanted to go on an early morning ride before heading off to work, so we started early. She continued to finish the loop and is heading home while I'm sitting in this park, waiting for the sun to make its way over a tall weeping willow so it can warm me up.

The activity in the park: fish jumping in the lake, squirrels chasing each other as they leap from tree to tree. The longer I sit still, the more activity there is.

Yesterday's weeding thought experiment was a success. After biking back to the house, I headed into the yard and started digging up the baby buckthorn. It was ideal weather for weeding. The chill in the air kept the mosquitos at bay, and the shade trees kept me from dripping in sweat. I paid attention to what passed for thought, focusing on the weeds, how best to pull them out by the roots. A week ago I purchased a knee pad and trowel. It was good to learn how to use them, so much easier when you have the right tools.

Soon the bucket was full of uprooted buckthorn, my self-imposed signal that I'd finished for the afternoon.

The best part was when Sue came home. She was surprised at how much of the yard had been weeded. I enjoyed her response, though I opted not to tell her that I had enjoyed weeding. I don't want her to get too excited about the prospect of me growing a green thumb.

What was experienced yesterday, being fully engaged in the act of weeding, is what Nishida terms "pure experience," which he says is "identical with direct experience. When one directly experiences one's own state of consciousness, there is not yet a subject or an object, and knowing and its object are completely unified. This is the most refined type of experience." The more direct the experience, the purer it is.

I've thought a great deal about pure experience, especially in regard to the activities that give me great pleasure: cycling and writing. It's why I decided to spend this summer biking to parks and writing, conduct that defines my personality. Now that I'm developing a talent for sitting still, I can include that in my repertoire of easily accessible pure experience activities.

But those are activities I naturally gravitate to. They help me forget myself and all the troubles and anxieties associated with "me." To have a pure experience while weeding buckthorn? That's certainly more difficult, since weeding isn't in my wheelhouse. My hope is that, by recognizing pure experience while enacting activities that I love, the ability to purely experience can transfer to those activities I'm not yet in love with, and in the process engender the potential for loving more activities.

I talk to my ethics students about Nishida and pure experience. I tell them that it's hard to do wrong to someone else when you connect with them, when you directly share a meaningful activity with them. To enact harm on someone else, you need to see them as separate from yourself. The more you connect with "other," the less "other" they are.

Nishida's Kyoto School of philosophy was criticized by some Japanese war historians for feeding the Japanese military machine during the Second World War. His critics claimed that Nishida's philosophy enabled the military to persuade its soldiers to commit fully to their cause, just as the military leveraged Shinto for its purposes. But I can't buy into the argument. If you lose yourself in "other," then how can you do harm to "other"? How could war be a pure experience?

The only answer I can come up with is that, if you don't know or love yourself, you could bring your own anxieties to the thing you're attempting to connect purely with. But is that possible? It seems that subjectivity, the "I, me, my," is at the root of discontent, anger, anxiety, all the trappings that prevent one from purely experiencing.

Japan is the birthplace of Zen Buddhism. It's odd to think that the Japanese war effort, its Tripartite Pact with Nazi Germany and Fascist Italy, came from the same culture. Harada Daiun Sogaku famously said that being ordered to march, "tramp, tramp, or shoot: bang, bang," was "the manifestation of the highest Wisdom. The unity of Zen and war of which I speak extends to the farthest reaches of the holy war." Holy war. The phrase to me is an oxymoron. The Japanese war effort was an outgrowth of extreme nationalism; it seems to me that nationalism is nothing more than organized cultural narcissism.

Is there a correlation between cultural narcissism and my learning to pull weeds? I believe so, because the more I purely experience activities such as yardwork or doing the dishes or scrubbing the floors, the more difficult it is to comprehend nationalism. It's simply a matter of scale, and the smaller the scale, the more one *acts* based on one's ability to connect to "other." The more one *experiences* it, the harder it is to plug into personal or cultural paradigms rooted in dualities, in one person's ability to view himself or herself as better than someone else, in one country believing it is superior to another.

Now that I'm learning stillness and silence, learning to quiet the mind, I'm realizing that silence is its own language. Is this park I'm sitting in a "good" park? Yes, if I'm able to connect to it, because as soon as that happens, I experience its goodness. No need to use words to judge or describe its merits.

I'm convinced that I'm living through tumultuous times, yet Nishida lived through a world war. He experienced the death of his first wife and four of his eight children. In spite of his ongoing, life-long losses, he still meditated and wrote poetry. He was as renowned for his calligraphy as he was for his philosophy. His poetry speaks of sorrow and of surviving his sorrow.

These ideas are beginning to spill on top of each other. It's "good" to write about, good to attempt to make sense of it all, but it's exhausting. I'm exhausted, and I've lost what tranquility I found in sitting still this morning.

35.

It's afternoon, and I'm sitting at the picnic table in my backyard. I just biked home from Herman A. Zeunert Park and had to sit down again, sit still again, and make sense of what I wrote an hour ago. What I wrote surprised me, the connection between a desire to engage in pure experience in daily chores and cultural narcissism and the rationale for nationalistic war. I'm sure it's a result of living through a pandemic, of COVID cases on a constant rise, of the social unrest, of the federal government's attempts to stem immigration—all of the narratives that play out on the evening news, all the separation and disconnect. Riding my bike back to the house calmed me down a bit. It's good to be informed, to know what's going on in the world, but it's also good to not be debilitated by it all. So much is happening right now that it can drain one's strength and vigor, and I'm doing what I can not to fall into that trap. Maybe this is why I decided, at this time, to learn to sit still: so I can take the time to develop perspective on everything that is happening, while continuing to live as functionally as possible.

I need to be functional for my family. Sue experiences the same anxiety I do when we read about the COVID statistics, the social protests, the presidential campaigns. We talk about it, which helps, but the daily discipline of sitting still helps too.

I need to be functional for my students. Classes begin in less than a month, and I need to be ready to teach them, especially the freshmen. They're going to enter a strange college experience, where they live in dorms but attend classes virtually, where they cannot engage in typical college social activities. Even though I'll be teaching online, from home, I need to present the best version of myself, to have the energy needed to get them excited about, or at least interested in, writing essays.

I talk about pure experience with my composition students. The first assignment in the class focuses on the students' writing history. They document who taught them how to write, what their strengths and weaknesses are, the whole thing. If they don't like writing essays, then I ask them to write narrative, to simply tell their story in writing. It's a great way to begin the semester, because we get to talk about why the students feel the way they do about writing. Most of them hate writing essays. I love to write them, in large part because I'm more familiar with the medium and can thus lose myself in it.

Is it possible for college freshmen to lose themselves in the act of writing college essays? This was the guiding question for my doctoral thesis. I observed six college freshmen for a year, watching them in their writing class, interviewing them every week, and examining their written work. Of the six students, only one had an appreciation for the writing class, and he attributed his appreciation for writing to his experiences as a stoner in high school: He was so baked in his English classes that he didn't learn anything, which enabled him to approach the writing process in his college composition class without any preconceived notions about how difficult writing can be. For the five who had no affinity for writing, their history focused more on diagramming sentences and had little to do with self-expression or defending an idea that one cares about. None of them had a sense of audience, of the value in writing in such a way that the reader would benefit from reading their work. Writing was always academic, always graded, always supposed to be accomplished in a highly prescribed manner. That's as far from a pure experience of writing as you can get.

It's harder to unlearn than it is to learn. To unlearn the negative experiences for the sake of having a pure experience of essay writing is a lot to ask of a college freshman. But I keep asking it of them, telling them, every semester, that the more they lose themselves in the writing process, the better their work will be, and the better they'll do in the class.

I'm teaching composition this fall. This time, I'll tell them that if I can lose myself in the act of weeding buckthorn, then having a pure experience while writing for our class is possible.

36.

I'm back at the Mequon Nature Preserve, though a good mile away from where I sat last time. The parking lot is full of cars, but my bike and I are sitting at a series of benches surrounding a fire pit, all by ourselves.

There are folks running through the park, walking their dogs, a mother and her two children enjoying the playground. Once again, I'm the only one sitting still and alone. The places I sit are not designed for single-sitting. Picnic tables seat six. This fire pit and its four benches could accommodate up to twenty. If what I do were a thing, Adirondack chairs would be part of the seating ensemble.

Yesterday, when I sat at Herman A. Zeunert Park, I focused on the lake, its fish and squirrels. There was other activity: people doing group yoga in a playground, an elderly couple playing tennis, more folks walking dogs and jogging. I didn't recognize them so much because I focused on the squirrels jumping from tree to tree. The squirrels were more interesting, possibly because they're what I've focused on all summer. *Homo sapiens* are a bit of a distraction from what I'm trying to accomplish. But these are public parks, and I'm developing a talent at putting the human drama in the background.

Simply sitting in parks still feels like an odd activity. I've traveled to this nature preserve countless times, but always with the purpose of walking the dog. I just need to sit still more and more and normalize it.

When I was in college, I kept a beach chair in the trunk of my car. I thought I could always pull out the chair, sit, and read a book. For the two years I kept the chair in the trunk, not once did I use it. What I'm doing now is different; the beach chair in the trunk was a designated reading tool. It would have been nice if I could have viewed it simply as something to sit in.

That wouldn't have been possible, though. The activity of simply sitting is inward, and I didn't know myself well enough back then to be able to delve inward. At this point in the lifecycle, I have a pretty good idea who I am, and I like that person. Which is a way of saying that I enjoy my own company, often to the exclusion of others. It's not arrogance or narcissism, just self-awareness – though, admittedly, it might sound arrogant to say that I'm self-aware.

When I come to this nature preserve to walk the dog, the activity is external: I'm with Sue and our dog Rush, and the focus is on the conversation I'm having with Sue and the euphoria Rush experiences as he sniffs out frogs and rabbits. There's nothing wrong with walking the dog, with sharing a morning with my wife and best friend. It just fulfills a different purpose.

If the person I am now met the person I was when I was in college and suggested using the chair to just sit, I would have thought I was nuts. Just sit? The twenty-one-year-old me wouldn't have been able to do it. It was hard enough for me to sit still long enough to read for a few hours at a time.

If someone were to watch me do this, they'd probably see it as unproductive, as if I'm not accomplishing anything, which is far from the truth. The daily ritual of sitting is intensifying other daily activities. Sitting still is requiring slow thought; it makes it easier to think slowly at other points in the day.

I can use this argument to rationalize the activity, though this activity is far from rational. It's emotional, intuitive. I wrote about this twenty years ago in my doctoral dissertation, where I focused on Nishida's metaphysic:

Through an emphasis on experience, Nishida's metaphysic interconnects intellect with feeling and willing: "The orientation of Nishida's philosophy was to shift from psychological experience unique to an individual to the perspective of a metaphysical system in which the individual is regarded as a part of a comprehensive whole" (Clarke ix). This is significant for those reared in western metaphysics because, according to Nishitani (Nishida's closest disciple), western thought often restricts itself to a psychological focus on the intellect (Nishida Kitaro 41) …

It's not much fun, rereading my own dissertation; my written voice back then was polysyllabic, academic, the voice of someone who communicates only with other academics. Yet the passage captures the gist of this activity I'm currently engaged in, an activity that, ironically enough, is as far removed from academic life as is possible, the university being what Pirsig calls the "Church of Reason," an institution that worships rational thought. What I'm doing now, in this park, is non-rational, richly intuitive: simply trying to perceive and connect with my immediate surroundings.

I remember the first time I felt a pure experience. Sue and I had just purchased our first home for forty-four thousand dollars. It was a wreck; we probably wouldn't have bought it if we had known what we were doing. But we didn't, and the seller did. The foundation was so full of lime that you could pull it apart with your fingers. Some of the studs were the same: You could take chunks out with your thumb. We worked for four years to fix up the house, while I was doing the dissertation, while we raised a baby, while I worked three jobs. It was too much, but at the time it seemed like we had to do what we had to do to get where we wanted to go. Which is ironic in retrospect, because we didn't have much direction, just a sense of moving forward, starting a family, building a home, taking care of each other.

One afternoon, I was fixing up an abandoned chicken coop. Behind the coop were a couple of vinyl seats I had taken out of the back of our Volkswagen Beetle. I was tired and sat in one of the seats and looked out over the farmland, the Palouse, a rolling landscape unique to Eastern Washington. I have no idea how long I sat there. It wasn't until Sue called my name, letting me know that it was time to fix dinner, that I came out of it. I sat there a while longer, having realized that I had finally experienced what Nishida was writing about. I lost myself to the place I was in. It would have been great if I could have ritualized that activity back in the day, but I had no idea then just how special that moment was and how difficult it is to simply sit still.

The purpose of sitting still is simple, but to get myself to do it, to ritualize it, has turned out to be a long, complicated process. Though I've studied these ideas for decades, it's not until my late fifties that I'm acting on them.

37.

I don't know the name of this park. It must have one; all parks have names. It's just off the bike path, has a small pond, a swimming area that, this summer, is not in use, and about fifty picnic tables. I've never seen anyone sit at the tables.

Sometimes it's difficult to simply sit, because I want to write, to take the laptop out of the bike's bag, fire it up, and write down thoughts. It's an activity I've done daily for decades.

The activities of biking and sitting help the activity of writing. It's good to find some physical and mental distance before putting fingers to keyboard. The three activities connect kinesthetically: the motion of bicycling with your legs moving but little else, the motion of sitting where your lungs move but little else, and then writing, just fingers clicking away. Not too much motion in any of these interconnected activities, but just enough.

I love rumination. The more the mind quiets, the more ideas pop into it. I put the ideas down on the digital page, and more ideas present themselves. All these ideas make up the essence of self. I decided long ago to define myself based on what passes for thought.

Our culture places great emphasis on appearance, something that has never made much sense to me. I'm personally content with how I look, the body I've been offered, but I try not to let it define me. I take care of it, a regime of daily exercise and healthy diet, get enough sleep, minimize stress. There have been times in my life when I gave emphasis to looking good, especially when it came to weight loss, when training for Ironman triathlons, but it wasn't the weight that defined me so much as the sport, the competition. Competing in an Ironman is as much a mental sport as it is physical, which circles back to Nishida, his assertion that you cannot control the external, only the internal.

Freedom comes from within. I turned fifty-six this summer; physical limitations now present themselves in real time. But I determine what I think about. I may not be able to bike as fast or as long as I used to, but I'm learning to sit still for longer periods. And sitting seems to help me think, in many ways better than bicycling has done.

I used to bike indoors on a stationary bicycle trainer in the winter, when Ironman mandated a nine-month training program with daily mileage goals. But it wasn't cycling. My kind of cycling demands being outdoors. Eventually, I bought a fat bike with a studded front tire so I could bike over the snow and ice through Wisconsin winters. The fat bike, compared to the trainer, is a better tool for thought: I think better outdoors.

A friend taught me years ago that "There's no such thing as bad weather—just bad gear." The saying gives you an excuse to buy quality bikes and cycling gear so you can bike in the snow, rain, wind, whatever's thrown at you. And the harder it's thrown at you, the more immediate it all is. Nature, the manifestation of the Divine.

Bike touring taught me to bike slowly; you can go only so fast on a fully loaded touring bike. Bikepacking taught me to go even slower since you bikepack on gravel roads, logging roads, trails, spaces that are often more vertical than horizontal. Sitting is even slower. Maybe going on bike tours and backpacking adventures over the last decade has been preparation for moments like this.

I had a great bikepacking adventure last summer. Because I planned on bikepacking with Evan this summer from Canada to Mexico, I thought I'd go on a shorter adventure to test out the gear and see if bikepacking was something I'd fully enjoy. It only made sense that I would, since it's basically bike touring in backcountry. I attempted the XWA, a route that goes across the state of Washington, from the shores of the Pacific Ocean to Idaho. It was the hardest week of cycling I'd ever experienced. The first three days took me through the Olympic Mountains. Nothing was flat. I had to rely on GPS to navigate the route, which was difficult since I'm so used to paper maps. Just knowing which direction to go was half the challenge. The next few days took me over the Cascade Mountains. Two mountain ranges in less than a week.

So much learning took place, so many "first experiences." I freedom-camped for the first time, where you just throw your tent up on the side of the trail instead of staying in a designated campground or park. I learned how to use bikepacking bags and travel with minimal equipment, since the goal is to travel as light as possible, to make it possible to cycle up and down mountains. I learned that you can't bikepack for eight hours a day, something I'd grown accustomed to with bike touring. I tried to bikepack all day, day after day, and paid the price on the fifth day, when I decided to pull off the trail and stay in a hotel in Ellensburg. The next morning, when I couldn't get out of bed, I knew the ride was over.

It wasn't that I was physically shot. I was mentally exhausted. I enjoy learning, but five days of learning how to bikepack was enough. I called Amtrak and changed my return ticket, moving it up a week and boarding the train in Yakima rather than Spokane. I didn't feel defeated for not finishing the route. I learned what I needed to learn: that bikepacking is serious work that asks everything of you.

Now I have all the gear to bikepack. My legs are as strong as they'll ever be. I just had to learn how to mentally adapt to the activity, and the best way to learn is to go out and do it, then reflect on what you did.

I love extreme experiences. I can recall every moment of the XWA, every turn on the trail, every person I met, every place I slept and meal I consumed. That one week provided enough material for a year's worth of reflection.

I don't know if Evan and I will be able to bike the Great Divide next summer. The route begins in Canada, a country that's blocked its borders to U.S. citizens. Traveling through small towns is just a bad idea during a pandemic, because of the risk of bringing COVID to communities that have minimal medical facilities. It's my hope that what I'm doing this summer, the serenity experiment, will be its own tool for preparing for the Great Divide. And if the pandemic continues, if there's no bikepacking happening for me for the next couple of years, then I'll always have these parks to go to and sit, an activity that's turning into its own adventure.

38.

I'm back at the Humboldt Park Beer Garden. They open in about an hour, so I again have the place to myself. Thunderstorms are in the forecast; the time to write may be short-lived. But I can still sit here. I brought a rain shell and hat in case it rains. There's nothing like hot summer rain.

I'm beginning to wonder how my students will respond when I tell them about this summer's thought experiment, all this sitting and solitude. I talk about it with one student, Veronica. We're reading John Dewey's *Art as Experience* over the course of the summer, a book she wanted to discuss because she loves art, and I love John Dewey's musings, so we agreed to discuss the book a chapter at a time. She's going to meet me here in an hour or so to discuss Chapter 5. It's a thick book, dense. Veronica aspires to pursue a graduate degree that melds art with design, science, and engineering. I told her that the book is more suited for a graduate class than undergraduate, which piqued her interest. She wants to learn how to read and think like a graduate student. Sometimes she can tease out the latent meaning in the chapters; other times, I provide an interpretation of the work. I tell her that it's not so much learning Dewey's ideas as it is learning how to read Dewey, learning how to sit down for hours at a time, making sense of dense material.

It's a good exercise for me too. I learned how to read such books in grad school but veered away from them when I found work in high tech. Instead of reading the same text for hours at a time, I read countless emails, reports, and specification documents. The material was chunked into small bits, not long and drawn out. Duggan would say that I jumped into a career that emphasized expert intuition, not strategic intuition.

All of the course texts I'm requiring students to read this fall term are long, 400 to 800 pages. I want them to delve deep into the readings, to spend time with them, to come back to class prepared to discuss and ask questions.

I'm teaching a course in Creative Nonfiction this fall, and one of the assignments is a thought journal. All I ask the students to do is write; they are graded not on the quality of the prose but the quantity of it. I tell them that you must write tens of thousands of words and sentences and paragraphs if you aspire to write well. They enjoy the assignment, like the idea that they're graded on writing more, not better. I do have other assignments that evaluate and assess the quality of their material, but when I talk with students who have completed the course, they always seem to remember the free-writing assignment where all they were asked to do was write, write, write.

Sustained reading, sustained writing. it changes the way you think. It helps you think critically, because you learn how to do the deep dive into text, whether it's your own or someone else's.

I want my students to learn how to be self-directed learners. By the time they graduate, they should learn how to read and write for hours at a time without someone like me requiring them to do so.

Not all the students are like Veronica. Not all of them want to talk theory, especially over the summer, reading a book that's not required. I encourage Veronica, telling her that the more you read theory, the less difficult it is.

I also acknowledged to her that reading theory in graduate school ruined my appreciation for fiction. I try reading novels, novellas, and short stories, but they just don't hold my interest. I get the value of fiction, the ability to empathize with a fictional character, to believe in a drama created out of the author's imagination. But theory just drove me into a deep dive into nonfiction, a dive I've never came out of. I'm grateful to have been influenced by fiction authors such as Milan Kundera and Pam Houston, Rick Bass and Ernest Hemingway. But those authors also wrote rich nonfiction. I've found myself reading their nonfiction exclusively, ever since graduating twenty-five years ago.

Not that it matters what kind of genre one embraces. I learned in writing classes that fiction writers rely on personal experience, and nonfiction writers tend to make stuff up. What matters is the quality of the narrative, if the prose is engaging, believable. What matters is that the prose enables the reader to sit still for hours, reading. Sustained reading is a skill I still work on; it's easy to let it slip, to put the thick book down and reach for the smart phone or laptop, to surf the Internet. It takes more discipline in the twenty-first century, all of the technological alternatives and distractions made available. It was easier to sit and read for hours at a time when I was Veronica's age, before personal computers and smartphones were available. But just because it's harder now doesn't mean it's impossible. I tell my students that it's more necessary. We need people who can hold onto a thought for hours at a time. It changes the way you think, shifts the kind of problems you can solve. Everything becomes bigger, because you can see the larger patterns evolve.

I looked up and realized that the beer garden's been open for about half an hour. I'm still the only one sitting here. The imminent rain must be keeping everyone away. I had best order a beer while I can. It's a good idea to put this laptop away, drink a beer, and wait for the rain to begin.

39.

I'm sitting at the picnic table in the backyard. Yesterday I biked home in a rainstorm, and the back tire slid out. As I shifted weight to prevent the bike from going down, I put too much pressure on my foot and tweaked it. it's too swollen for cycling shoes, so instead of pedaling to a park, I'm in the backyard with Rush, in the shade of the weeping willow.

It's not altogether a bad thing, taking a rest day from the bike, though cycling to a park does help the preparation to sit still, which helps prepare for the mindset to write. The whole process—cycling, sitting, writing—takes two to three hours. I'm adjusting the day's itinerary to allow for this ritual; it will be harder to continue this routine when the school year begins, though harder doesn't mean it's not possible. I just need to make it a priority. A stoic perspective would encourage this: do less in order to do what you do well.

I find that biking, sitting, and writing works best in the morning, before the day's tasks are addressed. It seems to make chores more doable, better paced. It's not that I'm doing them more slowly; rather, my mind seems to move at a slower pace.

Over the years I've developed numerous habituated behaviors. Some of them are in sync with the pandemic, first and foremost the need to self-isolate. Introversion helps in this time of social distancing. I just returned from grocery shopping and found it to be enjoyable, now that a new shopping routine is established: put on the mask before exiting the car, disinfect the cart, allow people to stay six feet away. It was weird at first, as all new routines are, but now it's normalized, and in a way I prefer it. I make sure to shop early in the morning on weekdays, when the grocery is nearly empty. It decreases any anxiety I may have about social distancing.

The most stressful part of the process is driving to the store and back. We decided last fall to become a single-car family, so we let Evan drive our second car out to Oregon, where he uses it to get to work. Cutting down to one car was a commitment to cycling more and a commitment to not leave the house as often. These new rituals simplify things, and simplification makes the brain work better. But the grocery we frequent is in downtown Milwaukee, which means driving the car, which happens once a week, and as always, other drivers speed and weave through traffic on the Interstate. I've changed my driving style over the years, spending more time in the right-hand lane, letting everyone else go a bit faster. Maybe I'm becoming an old man that way. Maybe that's okay.

I could do more to simplify. I could stop watching the evening news, though there's value in staying informed regarding the pandemic, social unrest, the presidential election. It seems we're living in a time of hyper-information. The president always seems to find a way to get a leading news story. It's an effective campaign strategy, using media as free marketing. But it's exhausting; it's overly dramatic. I would rather learn about the pandemic and the populace than politics.

I could spend less time on my phone, checking for new news stories on NPR, Slate, and the other websites I frequent. Spending less time with technology is simplification. I had a flip-phone for a couple of years, and that solved most of my tech addiction issues, but my employer started requiring dual-authentication to log onto the university's servers, which meant the need for a smartphone.

I work at a school that prides itself on its techno-prowess. Staying technologically current helps with job security, and it helps when communicating with students who fully leverage smartphone tech. Yet I often miss the simplicity of the flip-phone and sometimes wonder if it would be good to model the use of a flip-phone.

I struggle with the television, probably because I was raised on it. Most days I'd come home from school and start watching the same shows. During dinner, the television was rolled up to the table so we could watch Walter Cronkite deliver the evening news. It wasn't until graduate school that I stopped watching television altogether. Our TV broke, and we couldn't afford a new one. It took some time to get used to not watching it, but it gave more hours to each day to study, work on the house, and spend time with Sue.

After a year or so, my in-laws bought us a new television set. Sue and I agreed that it was better to live without one, so we gave it to a friend. A year later, my in-laws bought us another TV. I was frustrated by the gesture until Sue explained to me that most of what we talked about with them was television shows.

Now we have an entertainment room in the house, a big "slouch couch" and a 55-inch flat screen. I watch the news. I like to get up in the middle of the night and watch YouTube, which is a habit I should work to extinguish. I follow several brewing channels, bicycling channels, news channels. But I also find myself watching highlight reels of old Green Bay Packers football games and Formula 1 races.

Using so many electronic tools is not the wisest choice, but it entertains. Often, it helps keep things light. And I don't want everything in this time of pandemic and social unrest to be serious, concentrated, dramatic. Sometimes, it may be all right to binge a few episodes of *30 Rock* or *Arrested Development*. Sometimes.

PART FOUR

Relying on Peace of Mind

40.

I'm in the living room. Sue's upstairs in bed with a broken collar-bone, fractured rib, and countless abrasions. She was on a lunch-time bike ride yesterday, riding down a new road, rounding a turn, going from sunlight to shade when she hit a pothole, went over the handlebars, and landed hard on her side. She was wearing her helmet. Thank God she's just banged up. She had hip-replacement surgery several months ago, and our immediate concern was some-thing happening to the pins in her hip. X-rays showed no damage there, just other breaks and abrasions.

She phoned me, telling me she was on the way to the Emergency Room, where I met her shortly after and waited for the nurses and doctors to perform the examination. Over four hours in the E.R., wondering what they were doing to her. Now she recuperates, six to eight weeks of healing.

I didn't freak when she called to tell me to meet her at the E.R. I was surprisingly calm.

When Evan was eleven, he was hit and dragged by a car. Sue phoned, told me they were in an ambulance heading to Children's Hospital. I left work and started driving, only to realize, in transit, that I had no idea where Children's Hospital was. I ran stoplights. I was in no condition to help anyone when I arrived.

This time I was calm, sitting in the waiting room, surrounded by people whose loved ones are COVID positive. It's not the best place to hang out during a pandemic, but it didn't seem unsafe. I just looked out the window and watched the wind blow through the maple trees lining the parking lot.

I brought Sue home, made dinner, changed bandages, helped her get comfortable in bed, woke up when she woke up in the night to talk about the accident and what will happen with her work, brought her coffee in the morning, made breakfast, flipped the laundry, changed the cat litter, vacuumed the house, and sat with her on the back porch. For the next two months I'll be on point for domestic duties, and I'm happy to report, to myself, that I'm okay with it, happy to do whatever helps her recover.

I'm just glad she's all right, glad I spent my time in the emergency room gazing at trees. I had no idea this new habit, sitting still, would turn out to be so useful.

41.

The last four days have demonstrated just how slowly broken bones heal. Sue's second night was worse than the first; it doesn't hurt if she sits upright, but if she sits in the same position too long, her muscles spasm. The hospital gave her a prescription, a narcotic. We picked it up at the pharmacy even though she told me she wouldn't take it: She can't stand the way they make her feel. But around three o'clock in the morning, on that second night, she took the pill, wanting anything to minimize the pain, to simply sleep.

A broken collarbone and rib. If it were just the collarbone, she would be able to sleep on her side, but the pain from the rib won't allow it. She tries to sleep sitting upright, but as soon as she dozes off, her head falls back and she wakes up. We ordered a sleep pillow, more of a neck brace. It arrives in two days. We hope it will help.

Her injuries have provided me with ample time to sit, mostly watching her try to sleep. She tells me I don't have to sit up with her, that I should sleep so at least one of us is rested. But I enjoy keeping her company, even if all we do is sit in a dark room at night, listening to crickets.

I'm grateful for this thought experiment, the sitting ritual. It's so easy to sit with Sue. Yes, we'll watch a movie together in the evenings. I subscribed to a seven-day free trial of HBO Max so we can have some new movies to watch. But most of the time we just sit.

It helps that we've been married for thirty years. We know each other's company and don't have to say much to enjoy each other.

Half of the time, we predict what the other person's going to say anyway, which isn't a bad thing. Just deeply familiar.

The first couple of days, she moved about too much. She wanted to walk the dog, tried phone consultations with her clients, attempted to do the dishes and help with dinner. But her pain got worse, and she realized she needs to move less and heal more. I'm glad she figured it out; it's information that she wouldn't have received well from me. Healing means stillness, and being physically still requires some mental stillness.

I elected to "simply sit still" as a shift in lifestyle; she's been forced into it. At least it gives us something to talk about when we sit on the back deck, watching the birds eat from the feeders, watching the dog rest in the shade of the apple tree, watching the sun make its way through the maple.

She slept about four hours last night and feels better this morning, told me to go for a bike ride and find a bench somewhere, said "Go do your thing." Which I'm doing. Because it's been a few days since I've sat at a picnic table, I opted for my favorite one in Vermond Park, on the bluff overlooking Lake Michigan. The wind blows off the lake, the sun behind a fir tree. Last night was colder, in the fifties, so no mosquitos. So easy to sit here, enjoy a beer, a Good City Motto Pale Ale, good to feel a warm breeze make its way up the bluff. It's good to get away from Sue's accident and injuries, if only for a few hours.

42.

Sue slept through the night. She began in an upright position, propped up by pillows so there was less pressure on her broken rib. As we had coffee this morning, she told me she just wanted to lie down flat, something she hasn't been able to do for a week. She tried it, half propped by pillows, and to her surprise she felt no pain. Minutes later, she was asleep.

Sleep is beautiful. It brings out her beauty. As we had coffee, her conversation was animated, full of hand gestures. She told me about the night's dreams, what she hopes to accomplish today. I took a photo of her with Rush and texted it to Evan and Kait, letting them know she slept and is rested. You can't take rest for granted, something as mundane as sleeping through the night.

I'm at Lemke Park, a twenty-minute bike ride west of the house. The picnic table is surrounded by a dozen other picnic tables in an open covered structure. I had the park to myself until a moment ago when a Chevy Blazer pulled up. Its owner didn't exit the car; the engine's still running, probably to run the air conditioner. I'm disappointed, because the car interferes with the quiet of the park. But it's a public park; the car's owner has as much right to this space as I do. And it's good to see someone else enjoy this expanse of grass fields and baseball diamonds. I just wish the person in the car would turn the engine off, exit the vehicle, and quietly enjoy one of these tables.

I must keep reminding myself that public parks aren't designed for sitting still. You're supposed to bring your kids here to play baseball or soccer, or push them on swings, use the horseshoe pits or eat with family and friends at these picnic tables. I'm misappropriating the space. You're not supposed to quietly sit still. When I was a kid, I ran around parks like this all the time. When I was raising Kait and Evan, I ran around in parks with them.

Sitting still is not a dramatic activity, though the more I do it, the more drama is revealed. Little things become big things: the cry of peacocks in a neighboring field, the elderly couple holding hands as they walk the park's perimeter. The more I do this, the more I witness. And, as the dramatic scale gets smaller, the pace gets slower and details present themselves. Just now, the driver of the Blazer backed out and drove away, the quiet returned, and I smiled. A small drama, one I hope to carry through the day.

I'm reflecting on Creative Nonfiction, a course I'll teach this fall. The semester begins in a few weeks, so I'm working on my syllabus, deciding what assignments to give and which readings to focus on. This term, I'm requiring the class to read John Yorke's *Into the Woods: A Five-Act Journey into Story*. On the first page, Yorke states that your "character has a problem they must solve. ... The story is the journey they go on to sort out the problem presented." If I'm the protagonist of this park-centric story, I'd say the problem I'm solving is a lack of consistent serenity in a time of pandemic and social unrest; the journey I'm on, sitting and writing down thoughts on how to ritualize peace of mind, sorts out the problem.

A few pages later, Yorke writes that somebody's "got to want something, something's got to be standing in their way of getting it. You do that and you'll have a scene. At its most basic, that's all a story is." When it comes to this narrative, I have a want: to be serene, to learn how to sit still for hours at a time, to accommodate this activity so it influences everything else. The only thing standing in the way of my getting this is myself, if I stop this newly habituated behavior, if I let life's business override me yet again.

Toward the end of the book, Yorke writes that "if a character wants something, they are going to have to change to get it." I find that I've changed. I want to do this more and, as a result, do less.

Yorke doesn't demand that the story have heightened drama. It's easy to find material to write about when bike touring. Whenever you ride down a road you've never been on before, you meet new people, see new places, encounter situations you've never encountered before. It's easy to write travel literature: The drama presents itself. That's the core reason I love bike touring and bikepacking: not knowing where exactly you're going to spend the night or what you'll eat for dinner or who you'll eat it with. This sitting exercise, in stark contrast, has less explicit drama. How interesting is it, really, to learn to sit still?

The drama's internal, not external. The action takes place within, the change unfolding slowly over summer months, revealing itself every time I realize I've overstayed my time at a park. When I first arrived at Lemke Park this morning, I set the alarm on my phone so it would go off in an hour, so I'll leave on time: I need to drive Sue to work at a specific time, and I knew I'd be late if I didn't set an alarm since I'm learning how to lose myself in these spaces. That's a new problem, a wanted problem, a drama worth experiencing, the shift in this protagonist's journey.

43.

I'm at Mee-Kwon Park, just down the hill from where Sue had her accident. I thought I'd ride the route she took to see where she went down, to make sense of it. I've been busy taking care of her, too busy to give thought to what actually happened: her going through a turn, hitting a pothole, going over the handlebars, lying in the road on a turn, vulnerable to any car that might come up behind her. Her first instinct was to pull herself and her bike onto the shoulder. Once out of harm's way, she assessed herself, especially her hip, where she had surgery several months ago. She could tell that her collarbone was broken, but she didn't know until reading the X-rays that her rib was broken too. She waved down the first person she saw, a guy working at the golf course that the road cuts through. He helped her get situated, let her use his phone so she could call for a ride to the hospital, went to get her some ice. It took about half an hour for her coworker to find Sue; in that time, several cars drove past her without stopping to see if she was all right. I'm grateful that the first person that saw her after the crash helped her, made sure she was okay. It says a lot about his personality, anyone really who stops to help someone in need without giving it thought, just as it says a lot about those who just drove past her as she lay there, broken on the shoulder of the road.

Ayya Khema, a Buddhist teacher, wrote that we are defined not in how we act but in how we react. Epictetus, a Stoic philosopher, said that "It's not what happens to you, but how you react to it that matters." I talk about action and reaction with my students when we discuss Nishida, how he believes we're defined by our conduct, those actions that align with our values. It's cliché to say that we're defined not by our words bur our actions. What if, instead, we're defined by our reactions?

What's the point of having guiding principles if you don't exercise them? If you conduct yourself the same way long enough, habituate them, it becomes part of your personality. The best way to alter who you are is by changing how you behave, decide what to do and do it; eventually, you'll do it even if you don't decide to. The gentleman who helped Sue didn't give it any thought: He instantly helped, gave her what he could to get her situated and on her way to the emergency room. I wish I knew who that person is; I'd like to thank him somehow.

It makes me wonder how all this sitting still is going to affect my personality. Maybe I'll be more contemplative. Maybe I'll continue to see things that were less obvious before this thought experiment started. I'm grateful that it's taken no effort, no thought, to help Sue this last week, to help her get comfortable, get some rest, get her back on her feet. It will still take a month or two for her to heal, but she's already talking about getting back on the bike. She had me take her bike to the shop to make sure it's fit to ride. I love this about Sue, her desire to get back on the bike and ride.

I don't like the thought of her getting in an accident, going over the bars, lying in the road. But it's part of cycling. She was smart: She wore her helmet, which was cracked in the crash. Cycling is not an inherently safe activity. Even going down the bike path, in a time of pandemic, with all these other cyclists who bought new bikes and don't yet know how to ride them, is a risk. Life is risk. But I believe in controlled risk, in minimizing the variables. You put on your helmet before you get on the bike, inspect the bike before you go for a ride, check the weather before you head out and adjust the route accordingly. You look for variables, get to know them. And, if you're fortunate, you'll see the pothole before you hit it. But that's not always the case; at some point, you're going to go down. There are smart ways to ride, and it's so much better to ride smart than not to ride at all.

44.

I'm at Doctor's Park. It's a bit of a ride from the house but well worth it, on a bluff above Lake Michigan, a park large enough to handle all the people enjoying the afternoon. Mothers playing with children, three teens throwing a football around, kids swinging in the playground. It's a good mix: it doesn't feel like we're in a pandemic. We are collectively outside, so there's less need to wear masks, and everyone abides by social distancing. This could be as "normal" as you can get in a time of COVID-19. Maybe we've been living in the pandemic long enough that we can follow the rules without a sense of social unease. Maybe we're learning how to do this.

I again feel a bit on the perimeter—not of the park's perimeter so much as of everyone in it, the only one here sitting by himself. It doesn't bother me; it's just more of a self-observation. This thing I'm doing isn't being done by others. I'll just have to continue to do it until it too feels like my own, personal new normal. I'll continue to tell myself that I'm enjoying the park like everyone else in the park, just in a different way.

I don't have many friends. I've lived in Wisconsin for seventeen years, and the only friendship I've made here that sticks, that grows, is the one I have with Mark Zimmerman. My friend Jay lives in Hong Kong, my friend Denny lives in Washington State, my friend

Robin lives in Hawaii—old friends that I stay in contact with, just a handful of friends.

The thing that Mark, Jay, Denny, and Robin have in common is a strong sense of self-awareness. These people know who they are. They've done the hard work of looking inside and working their personas. It's a pleasure to see them when I get to, which isn't often enough. I'm lucky Mark wants to get together once a week in the summer, that sitting outside on a nice long bench works in this pandemic.

I enjoy my friendships, and I enjoy being alone. This serenity thought experiment provides permission to design a lifestyle rich in introversion. Introversion is a quality that my handful of friends have in common, a quality in their personalities that I find attractive. The topics we discuss require contemplation and forethought. I phone Robin every weekend to talk about reading and writing because, like me, he's a reader and writer. Mark and I talk about poetry and all things related to poetic aesthetic. Denny and I email daily about the metaphysics of cycling; he's the person who helped me make the deep dive into cycling two decades ago. Mark, Robin, Denny: If there's one quality they all share, I'd have to say that they're introverted, self-aware, and rather serene.

And Jay, well, Jay's an old friend. His lifestyle as a VP of a major global corporation doesn't take him down the path of serenity or solitude. He's sleep-deprived, stressed, and constantly stimulated. But we go way back, and much of who I used to be is wrapped up in who he used to be. We've grown in different ways over the span of our forty-year friendship, yet we continue to be friends. In fact, what I like about my friendship with Jay is how different we are, yet we're the best of friends.

If I desire peace of mind, then I should surround myself with serene people—and Jay. I'm intentional about community, the people I communicate with. I'm attracted to the introverted, the contemplative. The older the friendships get, the deeper they go. I probably won't see any of them until the pandemic ends; that doesn't put the friendships at risk. They've gone on too long. We've figured out how to keep the friendships moving forward despite the distance.

45.

It's early in the morning. Normally, Sue and I have coffee and talk. It's how we start every day. But she's sleeping, and sleep hasn't come easy for her since the accident, so I'm letting her get the good rest. I'll make another pot of coffee when she wakes up, and we'll have our morning conversation. It's good to see her recover. Every day she gets a bit better, can move a little more, take less pain medication. After thirty years of having coffee together in the morning, it's odd having coffee alone. And though it would be nice if she were awake, I'm enjoying coffee alone.

Five years ago, when I rode my bike from Seattle to Milwaukee, I wanted to learn how to bike tour. But the touring was simply a vehicle for a thought experiment: I wanted to see what I'd think about if I were alone in the saddle for nine hours a day, for weeks in a row. I wanted to solve a problem that had been troubling me for the length of our marriage: I loved being with Sue, and I loved being alone, and those two things were often at odds with each other. It was a big problem to solve, and I decided that if I gave myself enough physical and mental space, if I reflected long and hard on the problem, I'd find its solution. The solution came, an epiphany, somewhere in the middle of North Dakota. I realized that the marriage and my desire for solitude don't have to be at odds with each other; rather, they can complement each other. When I'm with Sue, I prepare to be alone, and when I'm alone, I prepare to be with Sue. The two don't have to put each other at risk; rather, they can balance each other out.

Sometimes I wonder what life would be like without Sue. It would ruin me, to lose her. I might have lost her if she'd gone down harder in the bike wreck, if she hadn't crawled to the shoulder of the road before a car came around the turn. Nothing's permanent.

I don't think it's unhealthy to wonder what would happen if I lost her. If anything, it makes me appreciate what we have even more, because it's seemingly impossible to picture what life would be like without her. I'd probably spend too much time alone. It's difficult to imagine, spending too much time alone, just as it's difficult to imagine life without Sue. I tend to do things in excess, so I'd probably pursue a completely different life, one that's structured solely around solitude and serenity.

While cycling through North Dakota, I stayed the night at Assumption Abby, a Benedictine monastery in Richardton. It was a great experience, singing vespers with the monks, sharing meals with them for a day. They honor silence; they get it. But the schedule they keep, the daily ritual, I'm not sure it would work for me. If I were a monk, I'd probably take a vow of silence.

Silence is a big part of the monastic life at Assumption Abby. The monks use silence to seek God. They designate silent spaces and silent times of day to foster prayer and union with God. The monks acknowledge that silence is not easy, just as facing one's creator is rarely easy.

I understand why people take spiritual vows and live in monasteries, churches, and mosques to meditate with others daily, communities committed to prayer and spiritual contemplation. I enjoy going it alone, all this time alone in thought and non-thought. What I like about the "lone approach" is that I can do it my way, whenever and wherever I like. It just requires a ton of self-discipline. Sitting still is happening daily; there is a loose structure to it, but the time of day and location have some irregularity, which allows it to take on a degree of spontaneity. I'm not sure which park or picnic table I'll arrive at when I bike away from the house. The park I select affects the way I sit still. It's good to mix it up, balance the daily discipline with some daily alteration.

In this lifetime, I'd like to take a vow of silence. It could occur on the next solo bike tour. The idea of relying completely on nonverbals is wildly attractive. It makes sense to me that those who do take a vow of silence do it for spiritual reasons; verbal discourse seems like an inappropriate tool for communicating with the Divine. Whereas sitting outside, being still, saying nothing taps into that sense of the spiritual, the nature of nature.

46.

I'm at the Thiensville City Park, just fifty feet from the river, sitting on a bench swing, watching people enjoy the park's walking path: pushing strollers, walking dogs, or just walking alone. Sometimes I wonder what people think when they see me sitting, since it's a bit of an oddity. I wonder if the reason no one else is sitting alone is that they'd find it boring, if that's the reason everyone in these parks seems to have a purpose for being here, be it fishing or dog walking or playing with children.

I often reflect on boredom. Students tell me that the material I ask them to read is boring; I tell them that it's far from it: They just need to spend more time engaging the text, strive to go deeper to find its latent meaning. I tell them that the best part of reading dense philosophical text is when you stop, put the book down, stare at the wall, and let it sink in. That, I tell them, is when your literacy skills jump to a new plateau, when you begin to become a self-educated philosopher. I'll even do an exercise in class where I ask a student for a passage that's particularly dense, have them read it, have the class try to discuss it, and then ask them to stop the discussion and just contemplate. After about ten agonizing minutes of rumination, I ask them again for their interpretation of the text, and this time the conversation is rich. Hands are in the air. They want to build off each other's ideas. We break through the boredom with contemplation. To teach philosophy is to teach students how to sit still and think, focus their attention on a single passage, make sure they don't reach for their phones or laptops for secondary source material that will answer the text's depths for them. They can get there on their own, and for some reason it seems to work best in class, possibly because everyone in the room is trying to do the same thing at the same time.

There's an article in *Salon* by Luke Fernandez and Susan J. Matt, "America's inability to cope with boredom is spurring the spread of coronavirus." The article begins citing statistics from the U.S. National Pandemic Emotional Impact Report, which found that fifty-three percent of Americans surveyed reported being more bored than before the advent of COVID-19. They speculate that boredom is driving people to disregard the rules about quarantines and crowds. An article Fernandez and Matt cited states that we're entering a "new age of boredom," since the sources of fulfillment we once relied on are no longer easily accessible. Having students sit and ruminate for designated periods may turn out to be a coping mechanism for the pandemic, a survival mechanism if you will. But it mandates learning to break through the boredom, to sit in a place long enough that you begin to be the place you're in.

In *Bored and Brilliant*, Manoush Zomorodi makes a case for boredom. There's a passage where he talks about "cracking open a book, stopping and thinking about a sentence, maybe going back and reading it again. Giving each word a chance to wow or impress or educate you." He goes on to cite research that suggests Internet reading is destroying our ability to engage in dense text, how the brain's plasticity adapts to Internet text, where you have too much to consume, material that doesn't ask for interpretation or contemplation. Zomorodi wonders if it's possible to be able both to read deep text and to read online. They're two wildly different activities, and to be able to do both is a cognitive challenge.

The more the Internet has developed in my lifetime, the harder it's become to do deep reads. The Internet seems to create opportunities for boredom, that habituated ritual of reaching for the phone to check for new email, new news articles, new social media. The Internet's not going away. Bookstores may be going away, but social media isn't. Zomorodi argues that we don't have to throw away technology, but we must use it more judiciously, to be more conscious and conscientious of our use of technology.

Books are technological tools that simply move at a different pace. Philosophical books, written by the likes of Nishida or Nishitani, Tanabi or Suzuki, force the brain to slow down, and the more one engenders the ability to slow it down, the less likely one will be bored. Boredom is the result of fast thought, of not wanting the brain to do anything but consume more data. it's about managing one's dopamine levels.

I'm sure there's a stack of emails waiting in my inbox. There are courses I need to build before the semester starts in a few weeks. There's always work to do. But I want to put this serenity experiment first, to continue the daily discipline of sitting still, to minimize the stimulus, to be in a park where everything around me is real, not virtual, not a representation of reality. If I can do that, then I'm sure it will help my performance in my day job, and I'm sure it will continually alter what it is I do for work. Work will become more contemplative. I'll become less skilled at doing small tasks, and as a result I'll probably be asked to do fewer of them.

Most important, if I'm not bored, then it's likely my students won't be bored. I need to model the act of deep thought, encourage them to come along with me, show them the path that we can all go down together, tell them again and again that the best thinkers often get the best jobs, because they know how to solve problems, big problems.

But it isn't just about students learning how to learn so they can graduate and create intellectual capital for future employers. It's not just about finding a good job that lets you think about big problems. It's about finding a manager that lets you think as well as spend time staring out the window, letting those thoughts canoodle in your head. It's not just the solution to the problem, the product, but the process—the person.

47.

I'm on a bench on the edge of the river on the north end of Cedarburg. The park is a canoe launch and take-out. I've been sitting here for a while watching the fish jump, listening to crickets and cicadas, watching people get in and out of kayaks and canoes. It's more activity than I'm used to. It's a Sunday morning; when I arrived at this park, I was alone.

It took several hours of cycling to arrive at this park bench. It's only ten miles from home, but the route ventured out on farm roads, which encouraged pedaling slowly. Every half-hour or so, a road cyclist would pass me by. I go slow when melancholic, when I have no desire or ability to do anything quickly, to get anywhere in particular. The melancholy, the result of being out of balance, spending more time at home, taking care of Sue, doing all of the chores that we typically share, reassuring her that it doesn't bother me to carry the load while she heals.

It doesn't bother me, really. It's just tiring, and the solution for over-stimulation is to do what I'm doing now, biking somewhere, sitting still. It feels normal now; I've been doing this long enough that it's odd not to bike to a park and sit.

Sitting still is how Siddhartha found enlightenment and became the Buddha: just sitting beneath a bodhi tree, motionless, for seven weeks. The more I sit still, the more it makes sense how this activity, or lack thereof, is a gateway to enlightenment, breaking free of suffering, the cycle of life and death. The Buddha understood his true nature and that of all living beings. It was the end of his spiritual journey.

People canoeing and kayaking, cycling and walking through the park, talking to each other, talking to their phones, a park full of auditory motion. The more I sit here, the less connected I feel to everything that moves quickly, feel more connected to the jumping fish, the fog that's been perched on a rock near the river's edge for what seems like half an hour now.

I'm judging others for moving quickly. I need to learn not to judge those who aren't doing what I'm trying to do, just as I know this frog doesn't judge me for sitting on this bench beside his river. He's motionless. This is his way to survive, perched still, his green and brown colors blending perfectly into the earth and plants around him.

48.

I'm in a strip-mall coffee shop. It's far from an empty country park. Muzak plays in the background, a nineties track; somehow, it makes its way through my noise-canceling headphones. I used to be a fan of coffee shops, used to spend entire afternoons in them, enjoying the communal space, being around people while not interacting with any of them. Sitting in empty local parks is suppressing the pleasure of coffee shops. I've grown used to being alone in an open space. It's a habit I'm not going to let go of.

I'm killing a couple of hours while Sue sees her physician. She's had countless appointments as a result of the accident. Her surgeon, chiropractor, masseuse, nutritionist. I drive her from place to place since her sling prevents her from driving. I'm happy to take her to these appointments, want to see her heal quickly, but the driving troubles me. We gave our second car to Evan a year ago, and I made the all-in commitment to bicycle commuting, a lifestyle transition that was surprisingly easy to adapt to. I've had no regrets, no turning back. But now we drive from place to place daily, taking Sue to work and back, the appointments, the grocery store.

I don't like what driving does to my head. It's like this coffee shop. You're insulated by walls, surrounded by stimulus. Across from me are two men having a conversation about a funeral they decided not to attend, then about another friend that's trapped in Hawaii since you can't fly off the big island back to the mainland. I don't want to eavesdrop on their conversation, but they're speaking at full volume, again, through the noise-canceling headphones that aren't a match for their animated discourse.

Driving Sue has been disruptive. I haven't sat in a park for several days. I am returning to bad habits, waking in the middle of the night and going downstairs to watch a couple of hours of YouTube, reaching for my phone every ten minutes or so to check for new email or news stories. It's made me surlier, certainly more melancholic.

I need to get out of the coffee shop and back in the parks, out of the car and back on the bike. Sue's accident was two and a half weeks ago; her recovery will take six to eight weeks. I need to be patient, or I need to have a conversation with her, explain that the moodiness is the result of all this time indoors and in the car. Though if I do, she may feel responsible. I know she feels bad that she can't contribute around the house. It's on me to prepare meals and clean up, keep the house clean, care for the animals. I don't do it as well as she does; I never have. I'm trying, but I'd rather be outside of the house than in it.

Sue's always been focused on our domestic life, while I've always focused on adventures and travel. She wants to purchase new furniture, budget for alterations to the yard, a new fireplace or raised-bed gardens, whereas I'd rather invest in bicycles, camping gear, airplane tickets. We balance each other out; our disparate interests ensure that, when we do come home from an adventure, we return to a good home.

But we're in a pandemic. There is no travel, no adventures this summer. We did go to Minnesota to visit Kait and Sophie, squeezed in a day of gravel cycling outside of Northfield one morning. It was a ton of fun, but it just made me want more, made me want to keep going down those long Minnesota country roads. I can't have what I want right now. I need to be grateful for Sue, for the time and intention she's put into our life at home, since home is where we are for the foreseeable future.

I need to get back into the parks. It's late August. The leaves are just starting to turn color and drop. The colder it gets, the fewer folks use parks. I have plans for cycling in my winter gear, wearing layers of clothes so I can sit still outdoors in winter. Maybe I'll get a portable space heater. Maybe I'll target shelters in the parks to stay protected from the elements.

It's good to imagine life continuing in a heightened state of balance, being at home with Sue while cycling off to all the parks I've become familiar and comfortable with. I need to remind myself of Pirsig's quote: "Peace of mind isn't at all superficial. ... The ultimate test's always your own serenity." I'm not serene, but the good news is that I want it back.

49.

Lemke Park. I came here hoping it would be empty, but instead there are a dozen children in the playground, a group of high school runners training for the coming cross-country season, and several county workers mowing the acres of grass. I need to learn how to find solitude in the presence of others. Most of Wisconsin is farmland and small towns, thousands of acres of corn and soybeans, but I live too close to Milwaukee to enjoy the open emptiness most of the state offers.

I did enjoy cycling on farm roads to arrive at the park. I took the "Rustic Road Loop." There are two miles of gravel road on the loop, the only gravel road in the county, and my bike loves gravel, is made for gravel. A steel frame, carbon fork, carbon seat-post, carbon crank, 1x11 SRAM drive train, 650b tubeless tires—it loves gravel. While riding those two miles I saw a dozen turkey, a couple of herons, a field of cattle, and hovering turkey vultures. All that on a short rustic road, and all this humanity at Lemke Park. I need to learn how to be alone in the presence of others, need to not be bothered by their presence.

I'd move to an emptier place if I could, go back west where I'm from, live in the mountains of Idaho or the rolling Palouse of eastern Washington. But I love my academic job, love teaching, and when it comes to academia, you go where the job takes you, you're lucky if you find work. And seventeen years ago, I found work in Milwaukee.

I'm rereading Gretel Ehrlich's *The Solace of Open Spaces*, a collection of essays about living in Wyoming. She moved to Wyoming from California because she had "suffered a tragedy and made a drastic geographical and cultural move fairly baggageless." I admire her, the ability to move to an open space, the emptiest state in the Lower Forty-eight.

When I was in my early twenties, I moved to Alaska to pursue an MFA in Creative Writing. I had graduated from college years before and missed being in an English Department, where you can sit in a room with other people who were reading the same books you were reading and talk about them, write essays about them. The program provided a writing community, graduate students who wanted to write poems and short stories, to read and write and talk about books and share each other's work. All of that taking place in Fairbanks, where there is nearly nothing to the west, north, and east, where you have to drive seven hours south to get to Anchorage. Three years in Alaska.

Sue moved up to live with me. We shared a one-room cabin that had no running water. It was tough and wonderful. We lived on a slough that dumped into the Tanana River. In winter, we could walk down the frozen slough and onto the Tanana. You could walk all the way to the Yukon if you wanted, if you knew what you were doing, all the way to the Bering Sea. I fell in love with all the space, the emptiness, the quiet I haven't found anywhere else.

Sue found work as a veterinary technician, worked for Doctor VanPelt, who worked on sled dogs owned by the best Iditarod racers. It was the early nineties; Vanpelt would let Sue do some minor surgeries, run the anesthesia, all kinds of things that you'd now need a veterinary degree to do. Which is why she decided to get a degree in veterinary medicine, why we left Alaska when I graduated.

I wanted to stay, but she did me a favor by moving to Alaska in the first place. It was her turn to decide where we would go next, and she opted for eastern Washington, where she would receive a veterinary degree after six years of study.

Eastern Washington was wonderfully empty, but not as empty as the interior of Alaska. After our time in eastern Washington, we moved to an island near Seattle; it was empty too, but not as empty. Then we moved to Wisconsin.

I miss empty, open space. I miss looking at mountains, knowing there's more open space behind them.

Every year I go on a tour out west, to be in open places and meet people who live in open space. I bring those experiences back to Wisconsin and work for another nine months, another academic year, and plan for the next bike tour out west.

It's a balance, living here and going out there. It's a balance to be in this park with others. I cannot rely on geography for serenity. I need to find it regardless of location, need to rely on the interior more than the exterior. Though it certainly helps to bike through Montana or North Dakota, cycling for hours without seeing another human being, fewer cars, fewer ranches, like going back in time, back when there was less humanity and more of everything else.

50.

A beautiful morning. It's nearly September: you can smell it. Leaves are falling, a strong breeze ripples across the pond. I'm in Brown Deer Park, at a table I've wanted to enjoy all summer, saving it for a special day, and today feels special. I love fall, which is to say I'm not fond of heat and humidity. Having grown up on the West Coast, I still struggle with humidity, the heavy air, the sweat that can form on my hands from the simple activity of typing on a keyboard. But not this morning. The sun makes its way to the sky's zenith, yet it's not hot, just bright, sharpness everywhere.

The park is full of activity. To the north, a catering group sets up hundreds of chairs for an outdoor wedding. Just south, lines of golfers wait to tee up on the eighth fairway, and frisbee golfers go by in droves. A photographer points his long lens at everything taking place. A father and son fish from a bridge.

Meanwhile, I'm writing. I love bringing the laptop to these parks to document what thoughts present themselves. The sitting exercise seems to bring out all kinds of ideas, especially those related to peace of mind, since the goal this summer is to discover a serenity method. It seems like I've found it, and it's simple: biking, sitting, writing. It takes time, a solid three hours: one for cycling to the park and back, another for sitting still, a third for documenting thought. In the past I didn't have three-hour blocks, was busy raising kids, learning how to be a good husband, a better professor. It's not as if

I have more time now. Summer has added flexibility, but that came to an end with Sue's accident. In a week I'll be teaching again and, coupled with Sue's recovery, time will be in short supply. Yet I know I won't let this go. It's just too good and has too good a ripple effect on everything else.

Last night Sue thanked me for making dinner, cleaning the house, and driving her to her doctor's appointments. I jokingly said, "It's serendipitous that you had your accident deep into my serenity experiment." I believe in serendipity, how things happen at a designated time for a specific reason. I believe that serendipity exists once you believe in serendipity. Does it exist only if you believe in it, if you look for it knowing it's there?

I am grateful that Sue's accident happened when it did. It hasn't been a struggle to help her recover. It hasn't been easy, especially the sleeplessness she experiences, unable to rest with a broken rib pressured by the sling that immobilizes her shoulder blade. Less sleep becomes grumpiness, her frustration with the inability to do what she loves to do, be it work or just going for a bike ride.

When I do get irritated with her, when I lack empathy, I try to check the ego, recognize that it's not her that's behaving poorly so much as my poor reactions. That ability to recognize it when it happens is the result of these sitting exercises. More space, more time outside, regular solitude, just feeling this breeze and watching the heron across the pond. Having this daily lets me rely on it, lets me bring it back home.

The world remains in states of chaos. Pandemic numbers continue to rise, social unrest and protests daily shed light on systemic racism, and to top it off, the Democratic and Republican National Conventions just took place. So much conflict. Yet here I sit in this park, beside this pond, watching a heron watch me.

We learn to live in trying times. Wearing a mask and social distancing are more normal now. I continue to learn about racism, classism, the privilege I experience just in the fact that I can enjoy sitting still this quiet morning. Sitting still helps with it all. Sitting still puts the world's drama and conflicts in perspective.

Writing thoughts down helps give perspective too, documenting reflections, rereading the summer's thought processes, learning what I'm learning. It would be different if I sat still and didn't write afterward. I'd still benefit from sitting still, sinking into serenity. But it's good to couple it with writing, the daily explanation as to why I'm doing this, why I'm sitting here.

A flock of honkers just landed on the pond, then swim by as if I were not here.

PART FIVE

Acting without Acting

51.

I biked to River Barn Park, just a couple of miles from home, to sit at a picnic table I found several months ago, but there were a couple of Little League baseball games taking place. I thought about sitting there and watching a game, recollecting the eight years I played baseball growing up. But there were dozens of parents cheering on the teams, and no one was distancing, and I still don't understand how it's safe for children to play baseball in a pandemic. So I rode on.

I headed west for five miles to the nature preserve. There's a bench with a shed roof that I sat under one afternoon last spring, in a rainstorm, walking Rush and waiting for the rain to end so I could get back to the house, back to work. That was a long time ago, just at the beginning of the pandemic, before I learned to sit still. Because that's what this is, a skill that needed to be learned and habituated. I love the word "habituated," because it infers that the behavior will continue without thought.

What an afternoon! I'm glad to be in the shed roof's shade, the sun high in the sky. I'm enjoying a Good City Motto Pale Ale, enjoying the breeze that ruffles the maple leaves. The parking lot at the preserve was full, and folks are on the walking paths, though where I am is hidden. To get here, you bike up a gravel road, turn onto a path through a wood, then onto a mowed walk that ends at this bench. Only one couple have walked past in the last hour. One of them looked at me and said, "Good place for a rest." I said, "I could sit here all day."

Indeed I could sit here all day. I did all my chores before riding here, and Sue is set up to do some work while I'm gone. It's a good thing I don't bring more than one beer with me when I bike and sit, especially at this location. I don't understand why I didn't sit here before. Maybe because it edges a bog, mosquitos thick in the summer months. Maybe because I didn't think you could ride a bike into the nature preserve; you can, but you need the right bike, and mine is made for gravel roads and forest paths. I'll surely come back here. It's just a twenty-minute ride from home. Easy to get to, easy to stay.

I tell my students, "Easy is good," and then tell them that the hard part is learning how to do something so well that it's easy to do. Like the Daoist concept of Wu Wei: "The Way never acts yet nothing is left undone." Effortless action. Actionless action.

I've been talking with Sue, often, about sitting still. She's been forced into it because of her broken rib and collarbone. I was forced into it because of anxiety about the pandemic and the summer's social and political unrest and protests. I want to be part of the solution to the issues we're living through; being serene is at the heart of the solution. I'm not angry at the parents and coaches back at River Barn Park. Several months ago I would have been: their letting their children ignore social distancing, no one wearing masks, behaving as if the pandemic were not taking place. But frustration and anxiety don't solve problems. The virus has no emotions.

I've found a way to maintain peace of mind. The mind wanders until it rests, the stimulation of life at home and work is periodically replaced with nature's stimulation. The sound of the crickets and wind ruffling the trees, the chickadees singing to each other.

I start teaching again next week, three months of summer coming to an end. But it doesn't feel like an ending, more like a continuing.

I will teach four courses this fall, will be in online meetings daily. But I've already blocked off two hours a day for sitting still. I may bike to any of the picnic tables and benches I've discovered this summer. I may just sit at the picnic table in the backyard. Maybe I'll hang the hammock. As long as the distractions can be managed, as long as there is enough time and space to find this mental place.

Made in the USA
Monee, IL
11 March 2021